ISBN 978-1-331-52370-3
PIBN 10028138

This book is a reproduction of an important historical work. Forgotten Books uses
state-of-the-art technology to digitally reconstruct the work, preserving the original format
whilst repairing imperfections present in the aged copy. In rare cases, an imperfection in
the original, such as a blemish or missing page, may be replicated in our edition. We do,
however, repair the vast majority of imperfections successfully; any imperfections that
remain are intentionally left to preserve the state of such historical works.

1 MONTH OF
FREE
READING

at

www.ForgottenBooks.com

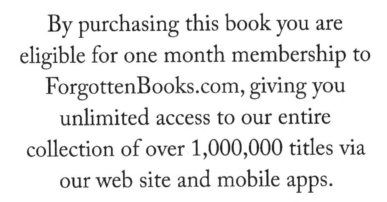

By purchasing this book you are eligible for one month membership to ForgottenBooks.com, giving you unlimited access to our entire collection of over 1,000,000 titles via our web site and mobile apps.

To claim your free month visit:

www.forgottenbooks.com/free28138

EX LIBRIS

ACCOUNTS OF EXECUTORS AND TESTAMENTARY TRUSTEES: LECTURES BEFORE THE NEW YORK UNIVERSITY SCHOOL OF COMMERCE, ACCOUNTS AND FINANCE

BY JOSEPH HARDCASTLE, C. P. A,. PROFESSOR OF PRIN-
CIPLES AND PRACTICE OF ACCOUNTS, SCHOOL OF COM-
MERCE, ACCOUNTS AND FINANCE, NEW YORK UNIVERSITY

PUBLICATIONS OF THE NEW YORK UNIVERSITY SCHOOL
OF COMMERCE, ACCOUNTS AND FINANCE, NEW YORK, 1903.

PREFACE.

This book has been written primarily for the aid of students. It gives in substance the matter which I present in a course of lectures at the New York University School of Commerce, Accounts and Finance. For the students who hear these lectures it will serve as a syllabus. The book, however, is more than a syllabus, and the general reader will, I trust, find it a

CORRIGENDA

Page 16, last line, change *has* to *have*.

" 23, line 26, change *distinguish* to *extinguish*.

" 45, line 21, change *18610* to *17610*.

" 45, line 25, change *1567.50* to *1642.50*.

" 48, line 9, change *receive* to *exceed*.

" 50, line 2, change *per. $100* to *for $100*.

" 62, in (7), change *Paid Transfer T $500* to *Paid Transfer T $50*.

" 62, in (7), change addition on Credit Side from *$2050* to *$1050*.

" 70, in (9), change *Paid A. Langstader $72.12* to *Paid A. Langstader $7512*

" 71, in (14), interchange debit and credit sides of account.

" 75, last line, change *54195* to *54159*.

phraseology. The chief sources on which I have depended are, the Code of Civil Procedure of the State of New York, and "Chaplin on Express Trusts and Powers," with the kind consent of the author of this latter work.

It must not be thought that this treatise will be of use only in the State of New York, for the general principles of the law are applicable throughout the United States.

Joseph Hardcastle, C. P. A.

New York City, October 28, 1903.

PREFACE.

This book has been written primarily for the aid of students. It gives in substance the matter which I present in a course of lectures at the New York University School of Commerce, Accounts and Finance. For the students who hear these lectures it will serve as a syllabus. The book, however, is more than a syllabus, and the general reader will, I trust, find it a source of independent help and guidance in his study of the subject. I have aimed to make it useful, not only to the teacher, but also to the professional accountant.

The book has the following objects in view:

1. To bring the lawyer and the accountant into accord on the subject, so that they may profitably co-operate in their mutual work.

2. To give the accountant such a knowledge of both the principles and practice of the law that he may do his work intelligently, leaving, however, the legal guidance, the procedure, and the forms to be attended to by the lawyer.

3. To bring out prominently the distinction between corpus and income.

4. To interpret mathematically sundry decisions of the courts.

It has not been thought advisable to include the "sale of real estate for payment of debts," since that subject pertains to the surrogate.

With respect to the law portion, it is more a compilation than an original work, as I deem it better to give it in approved competent language than to give it less effectively in my own phraseology. The chief sources on which I have depended are, the Code of Civil Procedure of the State of New York, and "Chaplin on Express Trusts and Powers," with the kind consent of the author of this latter work.

It must not be thought that this treatise will be of use only in the State of New York, for the general principles of the law are applicable throughout the United States.

JOSEPH HARDCASTLE, C. P. A.

New York City, October 28, 1903.

TABLE OF CONTENTS.

ACCOUNTS OF EXECUTORS AND TESTAMENTARY TRUSTEES.

LECTURE I.

CLASSES OF BUSINESS AND THEIR CONTRAST.

So far as Accounting is concerned, business can be divided into two great classes:—

1. Businesses which belong to proprietors and are managed by proprietors or by persons appointed by the proprietors for the proprietors' benefit.

2. Businesses in which there is inability on the part of the proprietors, and others are chosen, either by the proprietors themselves or by competent authority as substitutes for the proprietors, to transact the business in the place of the proprietors.

The subject matter with which the proprietors are concerned embraces real and personal property (either one or both), such as is capable of valuation.

The value is expressible in money.

Such businesses are organized, as to ownership, into the following kinds:

1. Under a sole proprietor.

2. Under general partners.

3. Under special partners, or under both general and special.

4. Under a joint stock ownership.

The subject matter of a business under the control of proprietors is called their assets, and is expressed in money.

The obligations under which proprietors are placed and which arise out of the business are called the liabilities. These also are expressed in money. In order to bring out clearly the two great classes of businesses and consequently to contrast them, we will explain the theory on which each of them is founded, as originating in the law.

(A) BUSINESSES IN WHICH THE PROPRIETORS ARE PERSONS
(NATURAL OR ARTIFICIAL) WHO ARE CAPABLE OF
CONDUCTING BUSINESSES.

The Personalistic Theory.

According to the personalistic theory, accounts are divided
into three great classes, according to the three classes of people
heading the accounts. The first class are correspondent accounts;
the second, custodian accounts; and the third, proprietor accounts. Correspondents are all those persons who are juristically liable to the proprietor or to the administrator of the
business for an existing debt; they are his true debtors, the
payment of whose debts the proprietor or administrator can
enforce by law. Correspondents likewise comprehend all those
persons who can juristically enforce the payment of the debts
which the proprietor owes to them. The latter debts constitute
the true liabilities of the proprietor. These juristic accounts,
accounts of true debtors and true creditors, comprise not only
open accounts with persons, but include all those debits and
credits of persons towards the proprietor not indeed headed
with the name of persons, but nevertheless debits and credits
of persons toward the proprietor supported by documentary
evidence, such as bills receivable and bills payable, and mortgages receivable and mortgages payable, debits and credits
which have taken the accounts out of the open accounts, and
placed them under other categories. It is not our business here
to give the subdivision of the only class of accounts which
are truly debtors and truly creditors of the proprietor. The
creditors are the true and only liabilities of the proprietor, while
the debtors represent the only persons who have liabilities
toward the proprietor. This term liabilities is used in the
strict sense of claims which can be enforced by the law.

We come now to the second, or custodian, class of accounts.
A custodian is one who is trusted with the care of property
for another; he is a trustee. He is called by various names,
according to the class of property he has in his charge. One who
has the custody of cash is called a cashier; one who has the
control over cash, a treasurer; one who has the charge of property, a storekeeper, or some other equally significant name.

The proprietor may be his own custodian, in which case there are two personalities joined in one. All assets not included under the correspondent class belong to the custodian class. The name of custodian heading each account has been gradually dropped, and only the kind of property over which he is custodian remains. Instead of putting Custodian of Merchandise as the heading of an account, we simply say, Merchandise, and instead of saying Custodian of Cash or Treasurer, we simply say Cash.

The word "debtor" of the correspondent class, meaning one under liability, has been idealogically applied to the custodian class; i. e., the use of the word has been extended to the custodian class, with an entirely altered meaning. It no longer implies a liability, but simply a responsibility or accountability for the goods entrusted to the custodian's charge; if they disappear he must be able to tell why they disappear, and show that it is through no fault of his own. The word "creditor" is also idealogically transferred to this class of accounts, with the meaning that the custodian is freed from his responsibility.

In all accounting in which the proprietor or owner is not the central figure, trusteeship prevails, and the ideas of the custodian class of accounts are dominant. The Merchandise account is the typical account of this class. The custodian is debited, in the altered sense, with what he had on hand at the beginning, with what he has received, and with all increase in value, under the name of profit; then he is credited with all he has parted with, and with any decrease in value or loss; and finally he is credited with what he has on hand at the true accounting. As the trustee has had a limited right of ownership conferred upon him, and as he is also custodian of the fund in his charge, consisting of all his assets in his dual capacity of custodian and trustee, he debits or charges himself with the fund, with all additions thereto, and with all profits; he credits himself with all transfers of property to others, with all losses, and finally with what he has on hand.

As to the third class of accounts, proprietor accounts, they represent the accounts of the proprietor as capitalist. The capital fund with which they begin is the excess of assets over liabilities or the proprietor's equity in the business. The proprietor in these accounts takes credit, i. e., he holds responsible the administrator who is debited, or held responsible for the fund of the business, resulting from the correspondent and the custodian accounts. He, the administrator, or the proprietor as administrator, is debited with the fund with which the business commences, and the proprietor as capitalist is credited.

You will observe that this fund is not a liability of the administrator, but merely a responsibility; hence the capital is not a liability, as is frequently stated. All increase of the capital fund which represents the fortunes of the business, belongs to the proprietor as capitalist.

From what we have said may be deduced the following rule: (a) Debit him who receives a value. In the case of a correspondent he becomes a true debtor; i. e., he is really liable. In case of a custodian, he becomes idealogically a debtor; i.e., he is answerable for the goods committed to his charge. (b) Credit him who gives a value. In the case of a correspondent, he becomes a true creditor; i. e., he can hold the proprietor liable. In case of a custodian, he becomes idealogically a creditor; i. e., his responsibility for the goods he has given out ceases.

In the case of the proprietor as capitalist we noticed that he became a debtor for certain values representing decreases of the capital fund, and creditor for all increase of the capital fund; the former signifying that for the losses he released the administrator, who took credit for the same; the latter signifying that for gains he put further responsibility on the administrator, who became responsible to so much the greater extent. Hence collecting together and making one general rule we have:

Debit him who receives a value or who of a value becomes debtor; and credit him who gives a value or who of a value becomes creditor.

We will give two illustrations:

Bought Merchandise for Cash $500.

Here the Custodian of Merchandise is debtor to Proprietor, creditor, $500.

Proprietor is debited to Cash, creditor, $500.

The central figure, the proprietor, is both debtor and creditor for $500. The proprietor's account is unnecessary, since it is both debtor and creditor for $500. The custodian of merchandise remains a debtor for $500. The custodian of cash is a creditor, i. e., is relieved of his obligation to the extent of $500. We usually say Mdse. Dr. to Cash $500. This does not mean what it says, for Merchandise is not debtor to Cash. But it means that as a result of the transaction, there remains an account to be debited $500, and another to be credited the same. Pacioli wrote it: By Mdse. ⋛ to Cash, signifying that the proprietor was creditor by merchandise and the proprietor was debtor to cash, the two carets showing the omission of the proprietor's name twice. Nearly a hundred years after, Manzoni wrote it: Mdse. || Cash. This is an example of debiting him who receives a value, the custodian of merchandise, and crediting him who gives a value; viz., the custodian of cash.

Again: Bought, for the use of the office, stationery from John Brown, $10. Here the goods bought were for consumption in the office, and consequently on their consumption the proprietor as capitalist became poorer, and the proprietor as administrator assumed a liability to John Brown. Debit him who of a value becomes a debtor; viz., the proprietor as capitalist, under that branch of his accounts, called Profit and Loss, and credit him who gives a value. Profit and Loss to Proprietor as administrator, $10, and Proprietor as administrator debtor to John Brown, $10.

Since the proprietor as administrator is both debtor and creditor $10, this account can be omitted from our books of account and it only remains to debit Profit and Loss $10, and credit John Brown $10.

LECTURE II.

(B) BUSINESSES IN WHICH THE PROPRIETORS ARE LEGALLY INCAPABLE OF CONDUCTING THEIR BUSINESSES.

In the place of the proprietor and the custodians of the first class of businesses is substituted the administrator of the business.

The administrator takes the generic name of trustee, and according to the duties imposed upon him, various specific names, such as executor, administrator, testamentary trustee, receiver, assignee, guardian, etc. In his powers he is subject to the source of his appointment, with such other restraints as the law may further impose.

As substitute for the proprietor, the trustee is the absolute owner of the trust property against the whole world, and is accountable to no one but the beneficiaries of his trust, this latter condition arising from his becoming a custodian for others. For the above reasons the estate under the trustee is called the legal estate, and the estates under the beneficiaries, the equitable estates. The estate of the trustee consists in the ownership of the property itself, and as such owner he can sue and be sued, and perform many functions pertaining to a property owner; while the beneficiary, by reason of his right, in a court of equity can compel the trustee to carry out the provisions of the trust.

There are three classes of facts affecting a trustee as a person of inherence and as a person of incidence, with respect to *jus in personam* and *jus in rem*.

1. Investive facts, by which he has become invested with certain rights and powers.

2. Translative facts, by which he becomes invested with certain rights and powers, at the expense of being divested of other rights and powers.

3. Divestive facts, by which, in consequence of being a person of incidence, he becomes divested of rights and powers which belong to him as a person of inherence.

The following arrangement of facts applies to trusteeship in general, wherever applicable; but it has more immediate reference to the trustee as executor or to the trustee as testamentary trustee, of whose account keeping we shall treat in these lectures:

(A) The trustee as a person of inherence, with respect to *jus in personam* and *jus in rem*.

I. Investive facts of trusteeship.
    1. Inventory of assets coming into trustee's hands.
    2. Increase from newly discovered assets.
    3. Increase from use of corpus.
        a. From rents.
        b. From interest.
        c. From dividends.

4. Collection of debts inventoried as bad, desperate or valueless.
5. *Choses in action.*
6. Liquidation of partner's interest.
7. From foreign administration.
8. From growing crop, the result of cultivation.

II. Investive facts, arising from translative facts, such as gains from sales.

(B) Trustee as a person of incidence, with respect to persons in interest, creditors, debts incurred for account of estate.

I. Divestive facts of trusteeship.

1. Losses arising from translative facts.
2. Debts marked bad or doubtful not collected.
3. Debts appraised as good which trustee is not able to collect, by exercise of ordinary diligence.
4. Funeral charges and testamentary expenses.
5. Articles of property perished or lost without trustee's fault.
6. Amounts paid creditors.
7. Actual and necessary expenses paid in management of estate, and execution of trust.
8. Amounts paid to testamentary legatees and next of kin.
9. Items of property remaining unsold or uncollected, with appraised value thereof.
10. Claims of creditors presented to and allowed by trustee for which a judgment or decree has been rendered against him.

On examining the above arrangement, it will be seen that the subject is divided into two grand divisions, the first of which relates to the trustee as a person of inherence.

(A) With respect to the investive facts, the trustee has a double relation, viz., as custodian and as owner. As custodian he is debited when he becomes invested with the facts, and as owner he becomes a creditor with respect to the same facts. Hence the following rules:—

1. As custodian of an investive fact, the trustee is debtor to the trustee as owner, the latter being creditor for the same **investive** fact.

2. When he divests himself of an investive fact, as owner he is debited, because his property is diminished; and as custodian he is credited, because he is discharged of responsibility.

Here debtor and creditor signify responsibility and discharge from responsibility as custodian.

If now we take the assets of the personal estate of an estate, and present each class of them as under the trustee as custodian, under the name of its category, and the whole under the trustee as owner of these assets collectively, of the personal estate, we have:

Dr.   Asset A.   Cr.
_____

Value (a)

Dr.   Asset B.   Cr.
_____

Value (b)

Dr.   Asset C.   Cr.
_____

Value (c)
     etc.

Dr.   Personal Estate   Cr.
_____

Value (a+b+c+etc.)

The accounts Asset A, Asset B, Asset C, etc., represent the fact that the trustee is custodian of the goods underlying these assets, and is responsible for their value, and the personal estate account represents the fact that he is owner of the same. As custodian he is said to debit or charge himself with all the investive facts. All the personal assets collectively are called the corpus, or principal, or fund of the estate, and sometimes the capital.

Often, however, it devolves on the trustee to take care of the income, i. e., that which arises from the use of the corpus, or of the real estate, as well as the corpus. In that case, as the income comes in in the shape of cash, he debits himself as custodian in the cash account, and credits an income account with the same, under some appropriate heading, such as Interest Account, Rent Account, Dividend Account, or perhaps

Beneficiary Account; and each one of these may be either a particular account, i. e., refer to a single beneficiary, or a collective account, i. e., refer to several beneficiaries, or to several sources of income.

Besides these income accounts, we sometimes have accounts representing the sale of real estate, when it is to be treated as personal property. In this case also Cash Account is debited, and Sale of Real Estate Account is credited for the selling price.

(B) We will now consider the trustee as a person of incidence. All those accounts so affected as to cause a diminution of the fund of the estate must be credited with the diminution, and the personal estate account debited with the same diminution, for the reason that the estate has not yielded the full amount of the appraised valuation, such as items 1, 3, and 5 of the divestive facts.

It will be necessary to debit the personal estate account with such items of the divestive facts as 4, 6, 7 and 8, as they become determinate, and to open either particular or collective accounts for the same, which will be credited with the items respectively.

Examples. Suppose there has been a loss of $100 in the sale of Mdse. The custodian account Mdse. has been debited with the appraised value, then credited with the selling price, and finally is credited with the loss on the sale, $100. The personal estate is debited with the loss, $100.

Suppose the funeral expenses amount to $280. The Personal Estate Account is debited with this amount, and an account called Funeral Expenses is opened and credited with $280.

We now have three sets of accounts:—

1. The custodian accounts, which are specific; i. e., they represent things which can be exchanged or handed over, and with which the trustee is debited.

2. The personal estate account, which represents the trustee, as the legal owner for all values of the corpus which have not been taken out of it to meet the incidences of the estate.

3. The distributive accounts, which also represent the trustee as the legal owner, but so distributed as to show how the distribution shall take place among the equitable owners, so far as it has at any time been determined. Distributive ac-

counts are of three kinds, one kind representing income, which arose out of the receipts paid in to the trustee for interest, rents or dividends; the second representing corpus which is taken out of Personal Estate Account, and has to be distributed among its class of distributees; and the third representing money received from the sale of real estate, when it is required to be treated as personalty.

RELATION BETWEEN CUSTODIAN AND DISTRIBUTIVE ACCOUNTS.

The next entries show the connection between the custodian accounts and the distributive accounts, or the divesting the custodian of his custodianship, for which he as custodian takes credit; i. e., the trustee credits himself as custodian. The cash account may be made up of corpus, income, and sales of real estate. When it includes income or sales of real estate, it is to be credited with all the items chargeable to them, and the proper distributive accounts debited with the same items.

ACTUAL DISTRIBUTION.

Debit the proper distributive account, and credit the proper custodian account. When the whole of the personal estate account has been carried to the distributive accounts and the whole of the custodian accounts transferred to the distributive accounts, the custodian accounts, the personal estate account, and the various distributive accounts will have been closed, and the trusteeship ended.

The above mode of keeping trustee accounts is that of double entry, and the books kept as posting media are the cash book and the journal, or sometimes only a journal; the book in which the accounts are kept is the ledger.

LECTURE III.

GENERAL SCHEME OF EXECUTOR'S ACCOUNTS.

It is not in the power of an executor to make his accounting in what ever way he likes, although there is nothing to prevent him from keeping his accounts as he desires. For this reason it is well to keep them by double entry, as given in the last lecture. The method of accounting is not governed by rigid rules, from which there can be no deviation, but it must conform to certain regulations. The method may be deduced from the code of civil procedure.

Effect of Judicial Settlement of Account. Section 2742. A judicial settlement of the account of an executor or administrator, either by the decree of the surrogate's court, or upon an appeal therefrom, is conclusive evidence against all the parties who were duly cited or appeared and all persons deriving title from any of them, of the following facts, and no others:

1. That the items allowed to the accounting party for money paid to creditors, legatees, and next of kin, for necessary expenses and for his services, are correct.

2. That the accounting party has been charged with all the interest for money received by him and embraced in the account for which he was legally accountable.

3. That the money charged to the accounting party, as collected, is all that was collectible at the time of the settlement on the debts stated in the account.

4. That the allowances made to the accounting party for decrease, and the charges made against him for increase in the value of property, were correctly made.

Decree for Payment and Distribution. Section 2743. "Where an account is judicially settled, as prescribed in the code, and any part of the estate remains and is ready to be distributed to the creditors, legatees, next of kin, husband or wife of the decedent, or their assigns, the decree must direct the payment and distribution thereof to the persons so entitled, according to their respective rights. In case of administration in intestacy, the decree must direct immediate payment and distribution to creditors, next of kin, husband or wife of the decedent, or their assigns, where the administration has petitioned voluntarily for judicial settlement of his account as, and in the case provided in subdivision 2, section 2728 of this article.

"Where notice requiring all persons having claims against the deceased to exhibit the same with the vouchers thereof to the executor or administrator has been duly published according to law, if one of two or more co-executors, or co-administrators presents his account and a petition for a judicial settlement of his separate account, he must pray that his co-executors or co-administrators may also be cited. Upon the presentation of account and a petition, as prescribed in this section, the surrogate must issue a citation accordingly. On the return of a citation issued as prescribed in this section, the surrogate must take the account, and hear the allegations and proofs of the parties respecting the same. Any party may contest the account, with respect to a matter affecting his interest, in the settlement and distribution of the estate. A creditor or a person interested in the estate, although not cited, is entitled to appear on the hearing and thus make himself a party to the proceeding."

The effect of a judicial settlement, as given in section 2742, and of the decree for payment and distribution, as given in section 2743, are very general in their character, yet sufficiently explicit to be a guide in any particular case. Different estates present different features and details, and whatever these may be, the account must present accurate, full, explicit and definite information and be given in a clear and lucid manner, so that it may be easily understood by all persons interested in it.

It is to be remarked that the accounting before the surrogate takes cognizance only of the custodian accounts, and these are all concrete and specific in their character. The acts of a custodian are investive and divestive; he debits himself with the former and credits himself with the latter, and the facts naturally divide his account into these two parts.

But the account proper must be accompanied by schedules, given to classify the facts which enter into the account, and to give all information necessary to render intelligible the condition of the estate. Each jurisdiction may frame its own form for the contents of the schedules, and the presentation of the account, but the various forms will necessarily amount to the same thing. The following is the substance of the form used in the County of New York, State of New York:

Preliminary: The date of filing of an inventory of the personal property of the deceased, and the amount of it as fixed by the appraisers.

Schedule A.

1. Statement of personal property as contained in inventory which has been sold, with the prices and manner of sale.

2. Statement of debts due estate as contained in inventory which has been collected.

3.   Statement of all interest of money received by executor for which he is legally responsible.

Schedule B.

1.   Statement of debts mentioned in inventory not collected or collectible by executor, and the reason why.

2.   Statement of the articles of personal property mentioned in inventory unsold, and the reason why; and their appraised value.

3.   A statement of all property mentioned therein lost, without fault of the executor; the cause of loss and appraised value.

4.   Statement that no other assets than those in inventory or in the schedule set forth, have come to the executor's possession or knowledge.

5.   Statement that all the increase or decrease of the values of any assets of deceased is allowed or charged in schedules A and B.

Schedule C.

1.   Statement of all moneys paid by executor for funeral and all other necessary expenses, together with the reason and object of such expenditure.

2.   Statement of the date when executor caused a notice for claimants to present their claims against the estate to executor at a certain place specified, to be published in two newspapers for six months, pursuant to order of surrogate, to which order, notice, and due proof of publication herewith filed, the executor refers as part of this account.

Schedule D.

1.   Statement of all the claims of creditors presented to and allowed by executor or disputed by him, and for which a judgment or decree has been rendered against him, together with the names of the claimants, the general nature of the claim, its amount, and the time of the rendition of the judgment.

2.   Statement of all moneys paid by executor to the creditors of the deceased, and their names; and the time of such payment.

Schedule E.

Statement of all moneys paid to the legatees, widow or next of kin of the deceased.

Schedule F.

Statement of the names of all persons entitled as widow,

legatee or next of kin of the deceased, to a share of his estate, with their places of residence, degree of relationship and a statement of which of them are minors, and whether they have any general guardian, and if so the name and place of residence to the best of executor's knowledge, information and belief. Schedule G.

1.   Statement of all other facts affecting the administration of said estate, the executor's rights and those of others interested therein.

In these schedules we have all the materials from which to make the account proper. It runs something as follows:

I charge myself:

With amount of inventory $————————

With amount of increase as per schedule A   ————————

With amount of income as per schedule A   ————————

I credit myself: Total charges   ————————

With amount of losses on sales
    as per schedule B   ————————

With debts not collected as
    per schedule B .   ————————

With articles mentioned in
    said inventory u n s o l d,
    schedule B   ————————

With articles mentioned in
    said inventory lost, sched-
    ule B   ————————

With funeral expenses, and
    other expenses, schedule C ————————

With money paid to creditors
    as per schedule D   ————————

With money paid to legatees,
    widow, or next of kin,
    schedule E   ————————

                                                ————————

                                                ————————

                                                ————————

Add articles unsold   ————————

Add debts not collected   ————————

            Total to be distributed   ————————-

to those entitled thereto, subject to the deductions of the amount of commissions, and the expenses of this accounting.

The said schedules, which are severally signed by me, form part of this account.

All of which is respectfully submitted.

New York.

....day of ......, 1903. ...., Executor.

This is followed by the decree of the surrogate giving the distribution of all the assets not yet distributed.

LECTURE IV.

DUTIES OF SURROGATES AND EXECUTORS.

The class of trustees which we shall consider is the class called upon to administer the effects of a decedent; viz., executors, testamentary trustees and administrators.

An executor is a legal administrator, appointed under the will of the personal estate of a deceased person, who has accepted the administration. The will gives the title to the assets, but it is requisite that letters testamentary be granted to the executors in order to give them such legal possession as the courts will uphold.

If there is no will or trust deed, then the decedent is said to die intestate, and the person to take the place of the decedent in appointing persons to administer the estate, is called surrogate, i. e., one subrogated to the rights of the decedent, in accordance with the powers and restrictions conferred on him by law.

Administration is the legal right to settle and control the estate of deceased persons, and also the exercise of that right. Letters of administration are the warrant, under the seal of the court, giving the legal right. These letters are of three kinds:

1. Upon the goods, the chattels and credits of a person (assets) who has died intestate.

2. Special letters of administration, authorizing the administrator to collect and preserve the estate, either of a testator in certain cases, or of an intestate (temporary administrator).

a. When there is a contest of a will.

b. Where a person of whose estate the surrogate would have jurisdiction, if he were shown to be dead, disappears or is missing.

3. Letters of administration authorize the person appointed by the court in place of an executor to exercise the powers given by the will of the deceased, called letters ₊of administration with the will annexed.

The functions of a surrogate are:

1. To take the proof of wills, to admit wills to probate, to revoke the probate thereof, and to take and to revoke probate of heirship.

2. To grant and revoke letters testamentary and letters of administration, and to appoint a successor in place of a person whose letter has been revoked.

3. To direct and control the conduct and settle the accounts of executors, administrators, and testamentary trustees; to remove testamentary trustees, and to appoint a successor in place of a testamentary trustee so removed.

4. To enforce the payment of debts and legacies, the distribution of the estate of decedents, and the payment or delivery by executors, administrators, and testamentary trustees, of money or other property in their possession, belonging to the estate.

5. To direct the disposition of real property and interest in real property of decedents, for the payment of their debts, and funeral expenses, and the disposition of the proceeds thereof.

6. To administer justice, in all matters relating to the affairs of decedents, according to the provisions of the statutes relating thereto.

7. To appoint and remove guardians for infants, to compel the payment and delivery by them of money or other property belonging to their wards, and in cases specially prescribed by law to direct and control their conduct and settle their accounts.

Administration in case of intestacy must be granted to the relatives of the deceased entitled to succeed to his personal property who will accept the same, in the following order:

1. To the surviving husband or wife.

To the children.

To the father.

To the mother.

To the brothers.

8. To the sisters.

To the grandchildren.

3. To any other next of kin, entitled to share in the distribution of the estate.

9. To an executor or administrator of a sole legatee named in a will whereby the whole estate is devised to such deceased sole legatee.

Letters testamentary and letters of administration relate back to the time of the decedent's death and legalize a payment to one of the administrators before they were granted. Executors may be appointed by implication, and are then called executors according to the tenor. A person may delegate to a person designated in his will the power to name an executor. A person named as executor is not bound to accept the office; he may renounce, provided the renunciation is made before he has intermeddled in the affairs of the estate.

The duties of an executor are the following:

1. To see that the deceased is properly buried, incurring only such funeral expenses as are necessary and reasonable, having regard to the estate and social standing of the deceased.

2. To have the will probated, paying such expenses as are necessary.

3. To prepare an inventory, and have the same duly appraised.

4. To realize, collect, and get in the estate so far as is necessary.

5. To pay the debts of the deceased.

6. To pay the legacies.

7. To make any necessary investments.

8. To distribute the estate.

9. To keep such accounts as will show how the estate has been administered.

DEFINITION OF TERMS.

1. The word "intestate" signifies a person who died without leaving a valid will; but where it is used with respect to

particular property, it signifies a person who died without effectually disposing of that property by will, whether he left a will or not.

2.   The word "assets" signifies personal property applicable to the payment of the debts of a decedent.

3.   The words "debts" includes every claim and demand, upon which a judgment for a sum of money or directing the payment of money could be recovered in an action; and the word "creditor" includes every person having such a claim or demand, any person having a claim for expenses of administration, or any person having a claim for funeral expenses.

4.   The word "will" signifies a last will and testament, and includes all the codicils to a will.

5.   The expression "testamentary trustee" includes every person, except an executor and administrator with the will annexed, or a guardian, who is designated by a will or by any competent authority to execute a trust created by a will; and it includes such an executor or administrator, where he is acting in the execution of a trust created by the will which is separable from his functions as executor or administrator.

6.   The expression "letters of administration" includes letters of temporary administration.

7.   The word "surrogate," where it is used in the text, or in a bond or undertaking given pursuant to any provision of chapter 18, article 3, of the code of civil procedure, includes every officer or any court vested by law with the functions of surrogate.

8.   The expression "judicial settlement", where it is applied to an account, signifies a decree of a surrogate court, whereby the account is made conclusive upon the parties to the special proceeding, either for all purposes, or for certain purposes specified in the statutes; and an account thus made conclusive is said to be judicially settled.

9.   The expression "intermediate account" denotes an account filed in the surrogate's office, for the purpose of disclosing the acts of the person accounting, and the condition of the estate or fund in his hands not made the subject of a judicial settlement.

10.   The expression "upon the return of a citation" where it is used in a provision requiring an act to be done in the

surrogate's court, relates to the time and place at which the citation is returnable, or to which the hearing is adjourned; includes a supplemental citation, issued to bring in a party who ought to be, but who has not been cited; and implies that before doing the act specified, due proof must be made that all persons required to be cited have been duly cited.

11. The expression "person interested", where it is used in connection with the estate or fund, includes every person entitled either absolutely or contingently to share in the estate or the proceeds thereof, or in the fund, as husband, wife, legatee, next of kin, heir, devisee, assignee, grantee, or otherwise, except as a creditor. Where a provision prescribes that a person interested may object to an appointment, or may apply for an inventory, an account, or increased security, an allegation of his interest, duly verified, suffices, although his interest is disputed; unless he has been excluded by a judgment, decree or other final determination and no appeal therefrom is pending.

12. The term "next of kin", includes all those, other than a surviving husband or wife, entitled under the provisions of the law relating to the distribution of personal property to share in the unbequeathed residue of the assets of a decedent after the payment of debts and expenses.

13. The expression "real property" includes every estate, interest and right, legal or equitable, in lands, tenements, or hereditaments, except those which are determined, or distinguished by the death of a person seized or possessed thereof, or in any manner entitled thereto, and except those which are declared by law to be assets. The word "inheritance" signifies real property, as defined in this subdivision, descended as prescribed by law. The expression "personal property" signifies every kind of property which survives a decedent other than real property, as defined in this subdivision, and includes a right of action conferred by special statutory provision upon executor or administrator.

We will now consider in order the executor's duties.

I. *To see that the deceased is properly buried.* Anyone performing the Christian services of burying a deceased person will be allowed reasonable funeral expenses out of the estate, without reference to the rights of next of kin or creditors, and in preference to their claims. An executor can even before probate dispose of assets to pay funeral expenses. These expenses seem to include expenses incurred for medical attendance and others of like kind.

For the purpose of preserving the property of his testator he may, though he is not bound to do so, take it into his own possession, and for that purpose may peacefully enter into the house of the heir where the effects may be and take them. And when the effects, at the decease of his testator, are in possession of parties not interested in the preservation of them, there can be no doubt of the duty of an executor to take and properly care for them.

II. *Proof of Will.* The application for proof of will may be made by an executor, devisee or legatee named therein or by any person interested in the estate of deceased. The petition for proof should therein show:

    1. The residence of testator and his death:

(a) That he was an inhabitant of the county of the surrogate;

(b) That not being an inhabitant of the state, he died in the county of such surrogate, leaving assets therein;

(c) That not being an inhabitant of the state, he died out of the state, leaving assets in the county of such surrogate.

(d) That not being an inhabitant of the state, he died out of the state, not leaving assets therein, but the assets of such testator have since his death come into the county of such surrogate; or

(e) That some real estate devised by testator is situated in the county of such surrogate, and no other surrogate has gained jurisdiction under any of the preceding clauses;

    2. That he left a last will and testament, with the description of it, if not produced with the petition.

    3. That it relates to real or personal property or both.

    4. The heirs at law, or the widow and next of kin of the testator, or that the same cannot, after diligent inquiry, be ascertained.

    5. A prayer for the issuing a citation requiring the heirs at law, or the widow and next of kin, or all of them to appear and attend the probate of the will.

The heirs of a deceased person are those who would succeed to real estate under the statute in relation to descent, and are:

1. His children lawfully begotten, if he have any, and the children of such as shall have died.
2. His father if he be living.
3. His mother if she be living, or
4. His collateral relatives.

The next of kin are:

1. The children and descendants.
2. The father.
3. The mother and brothers and sisters, and the legal representatives of such as shall have died.
4. His collateral relatives, not beyond brothers' and sisters' children.

The heirs at law and next of kin of an illegitimate are:

1. His descendants.
2. His mother.
3. His relatives on the part of his mother.

It is not necessary to enter into the details of proving the will, but only to remark that the expenses of the executor or other person who shall serve the citation, will be allowed as part of the expenses of administration, without regard to creditors, as well as the expenses of advertising in the newspapers. If there arises a contention in the proof of the will, delaying the proof, it may be necessary for the surrogate to appoint a temporary or special administration *ad colligendum,* that is for the purpose of collecting, etc.

LECTURE V.

EXECUTOR'S INVENTORY.

III. *To prepare an inventory and have the same duly appraised.* On application of an executor or administrator, the surrogate by writing must appoint two disinterested appraisers, as often as may be necessary, to appraise the personal property of a deceased person. They shall be entitled to receive a reasonable compensation for their services, to be allowed by the surrogate, not exceeding for each the sum of five dollars for each day actually employed in making appraisement, in addition to expenses actually and necessarily incurred. The number of days' service rendered and the amount of such expenses must be verified by the affidavit of the appraiser, delivered to the executor or administrator, and adjusted by the surrogate before payment of his fees.

The executors and administrators, within a reasonable time after giving a notice of at least five days to the legatees and next of kin residing in the county where the property is situated, and posting a notice in three of the most public places of the town, specifying the time and place at which the appraisement will be made, must make a true and perfect inventory of all the personal property of the testator or intestate, and if in different and distinct places two or more such inventories, as may be necessary. Before making the appraisement, the appraisers must take and subscribe an oath to be inserted in the inventory, that they will truly, honestly, and impartially appraise the personal property exhibited to them, according to the best of their knowledge and ability. They must, in the presence of such of the parties interested as attend, estimate and appraise the property exhibited to them, and set down each article separately with the value thereof in dollars and cents distinctly in figures opposite to the articles respectively.

WHAT SHALL BE DEEMED ASSETS.

The following shall be deemed assets and go to the executors or administrators, to be applied and distributed as part of the personal property of the testator or intestate, and be included in the inventory:

A. Leases for years, lands held by the deceased from year to year, and estates held by him for the life of another person.

The first division of assets relates to active leases. They may be called active because they are at the present time bearing fruit; i. e., yielding rent to the estate of the decedent. They are personal property because the rights under them are less than property in fee or freehold. It is very difficult to tell how the ordinary appraisers put a value on these leases; but the true value of assets of this nature must depend on the net income derivable therefrom, according to the best estimate of the same, considered in relation to the time the income will last.

They may be converted into cash by sale, or kept intact and turned over to the next of kin at the termination of the executorship or testamentary trusteeship, or they may lapse, the term having run out. If the profits from them, either real or estimated, exceed the disbursements incurred in consequence of holding them, then they have a value, but if the disbursements exceed the profits from them, then they are an obligation upon the estate.

A1. Leases for years. These are leases held by the decedent at the time of his death and are terminable at some certain future date. If we subtract the sum of the annual disbursements, certain and estimated, on account of property covered by lease, from the estimated gross annual returns from said property, we obtain the net yearly estimated value of the property of the estate of the decedent. This estimated net annual value of the lease is an annuity, and the annuity will last for the time of the lease. With money at say 6% per annum (for a high rate covers risks pertaining to lease), the present value of such an annuity will give the value of the lease. The present value may be calculated either by an algebraical formula, or obtained from a table of the present value of an annuity of $1 per annum, and is then often called the number of years' purchase, for the reason that the net annual annuity multiplied by the number of years will give the present value of the lease.

We will now give a few examples of the valuation of leases for years:

Example 1. When the lessee has leased the term of his lease at an improved rent.

The lease has 13 years to run, subject to landlord's rent of $500, average annual taxes $250, average repairs and maintenance $250. It yields an annual rent of $1,500, money being considered to yield for such property 6% per annum.

Estimated annual outlay, $500+$250+$250=$1,000.

Estimated net annual return, $1,500—$1,000=$500.

By annuity table showing present value of $1 per annum for 13 years at 6% per annum, we obtain 8.85 years' purchase, and $500×8.85=$4,425, present value of lease.

Example 2.   Take the same as in last example, but subject
              to rent charge of $100 per annum for 10 years.
              At 6% per annum this gives 7.36 years' pur-
              chase, and $100×7.36=$736, value of rent
              charge.

Therefore value of lease, $4,425—$736=$3,689.

Example 3.   A tenant hires property for $1,000 per annum
              for 21 years, the tenant to pay taxes and make
              all repairs. The landlord agrees at the end of
              the lease to pay for contemplated improve-
              ments $4,000. The property is rented at an
              improved rent of $5,000.

What is the value of the lease having 10 years yet to run, the
average yearly taxes being $800, insurance $240, the repairs,
maintenance, cost of collecting rent, and risk of losses on col-
lections being estimated at $1,000, with money at 4% for this
kind of property?

The present value of $1 due in 10 years at 4% is .675564.

The present value of improvements, $4,000, is

$$\$4,000 \times .675564 = \$2,702.256$$

Annual disbursements, $1000+$800+$1000+$240=$3040

Net rent receivable on lease, $5000—$3040=1960.

Ten years' annuity at 4% gives 8.11 years' purchase.

Value of lease without improvements, $1960×8.11
                                       =$15895.60

Value of lease with improvements, $15895.60+$2702.26
                                       =$18597.86

A2. Leases from year to year. These leases occur when
a tenant has had a lease for a number of years, and does not
renew it, but continues in possession on terms like those in
the original lease, except as to the term of the lease. They
can be terminated at the end of any year. They do not seem
to be assignable. In giving their value they can only be estimated as a one-year lease.

A3. Estates held by decedent for the life of another person. These are treated in the same way as leases for a term of
years except that the number of years' purchase the lease is
worth is obtained from a table of net life annuities. For example, the number of years' purchase of an annuity of $1 for
a person aged 74 at 4% is 5.124; of a person aged 15, it is

19.403; of a person aged 44 it is 14.159. The present value of a net income of $1000 of a person aged 44: $1000×14.159 =$14159.

B. The interest in any lease remaining in the estate of the decedent at the time of his death for a term of years after the expiration of any sub-lease granted by him to any other person.

We will illustrate this condition thus:—A, the decedent, obtained a lease of a piece of property for 21 years; immediately he made a lease of the same to B for a term of 10 years; 5 years of B's lease had elapsed when A died.

B's lease has now 5 years to run before the property reverts to the estate of A. The estate has an interest in the property, which after 5 years will continue for 11 years. This is called a *deferred annuity*.

Suppose the net annual income of this property is $1200. The lease has 16 years to run, the number of years' purchase for 16 years say at 4% is by table 11.65. The lease has 5 years to run before it reverts to A's estate, and the number of years' purchase for 5 years at 4% is 4.45. Therefore the number of years' purchase for the last 11 years is 11.65 — 4.45=7.20. Value of lease, $1,200×7.20=$8640.

C. The interest in lands devised to an executor for a term of years for the payment of debts.

This is not a lease for a term of years; but it is the case of a lessee in possession of a lessor's lease as security for the payment of a debt. The value of this is the debt unpaid, but it is not carried out by the United States Rule for partial payments. Instead, receipts from rents, etc., are applied in reduction of capital until the debt is paid, and then to interest due. (In matter of Tietgen, 5 Dem. 350.)

D. Things annexed to the freehold or to any building for the purpose of trade or manufacture, and not fixed into the wall of a house so as to be essential to its support. These are called trade fixtures or tenant fixtures.

E. The crops growing on the land of deceased at the time of his death.

F. Every kind of produce raised annually by labor and cultivation, except grass growing and fruit not gathered.

(Items E and F separate the produce which is the result of

labor and cultivation from that which is purely due to the efforts of nature.)

G. Rents reserved to the deceased which had accrued at the time of his death. (Accrued here is interpreted "in arrears".)

Of course rents in arrears are personal property, being merely debts which had become due but had not been paid.

H. Debts secured by mortgages, bonds, notes or bills, accounts, moneys and bank-bills or other circulating medium, things in action, and stocks in any corporation or joint association. These are documentary assets.

I. Goods, wares, merchandise, utensils, furniture, cattle, provisions, moneys unpaid on contracts for sale of land, and every other species of personal property. These are tangible assets. These, I am inclined to think, should be valued on the principle of replacement, modified by wear and tear.

SECTION 2714 OF CODE OF CIVIL PROCEDURE.

"The inventory must contain a particular statement of all bonds, mortgages, notes, and other securities for the payment of money belonging to the deceased, known to the executor or administrator; with the name of the debtor in each security, the date, the sum originally payable; the indorsements thereon, if any, with their dates, and the sum which in the judgment of the appraisers is collectible on each security; and of all moneys, whether in specie or bank bills, or other circulating medium belonging to the deceased, which have come to the hands of the executor or administrator; and if none have come into his hands, the fact shall be stated in the inventory. The naming of a person executor in a will does not operate as a discharge or bequest of any just claim which the testator had against him; but it must be included among the credits and effects of the deceased in the inventory, and the executor shall be liable for the same as for so much money in his hands at the time the debt or demand becomes due, and he must apply and distribute the same in the payment of debts and legacies, and among the next of kin, as part of the personal property of the deceased. The discharge or bequest in a will of a debt or demand of the testator against an executor named therein, or against any other person, is not valid as against the creditors of the deceased, but must be construed as only a specific bequest of such debts or demand; and the amount thereof must be included in the inventory, and, if necessary, be applied in the payment of his debts; and if not necessary for that purpose, must be paid in the same manner and proportion as other specific legacies. If personal property not mentioned in any inventory come to the possession or knowledge of an executor or administrator, he must cause the same to be appraised as herein required, and an inventory thereof to be returned within two months after the discovery thereof, and the making of such inventory and return may be enforced in the same manner as in the case of a first inventory."

Upon the completion of the inventory duplicates must be made and signed by the appraisers, one of which must be retained by the executor and the other returned to the surrogate's office within three months of the date of grant of the letters testamentary.

The inventory is *prima facie* evidence of the value of the estate. Any increase over the values therein stated belongs to the estate and any decrease must be explained in the accounting.

An executor should supply himself with a true copy of the will when he enters on his duties, and he should carefully follow its directions in the exercise of his duties, looking for advice to his attorney on all points which are not easily understood by himself.

Unless real estate is devised to an executor in trust, the heir or devisee is the only person who has the right to its possession, except where it may be required to pay debts of the decedent, and the executor as such has no control over it; he receives his authority from the will or statute.

The title to real estate will vest in a testamentary trustee, and he is accountable for the proceeds of such real estate upon a sale, but he should not make such sales without first consulting his attorney.

IV. To Realize, Collect, and Get in the Estate.

If an executor or administrator discover that the debts against any deceased person and the legacies bequeathed by him cannot be paid and satisfied without a sale of the personal property of the deceased, the same, so far as may be necessary for the payment of such debts and legacies, must be sold (see section 2717).

The executor so far is a person of inherence, that is, the property inheres in him, or he is considered the owner who is given the legal right to obtain the possession of it.

LECTURE VI.

DISTRIBUTION OF ASSETS AND PRINCIPLES OF BOOKKEEPING.

Next after gathering together the assets, the executor should distribute the same according to the last will and testament modified by law. However, the will is the chief directing power so long as it is able, according to law, to be the executor's guide.

In the distribution the executor must fortify himself with the vouchers. On an accounting by an executor or administrator, the accounting party must file a voucher for every payment, excepting in one of the following cases:

1. For any proper item of expenditure not exceeding $20, if it is supported by his own uncontradicted oath, stating positively the fact of the payment, and when and to whom the payment was made; but all the items so allowed against an estate shall not exceed $500.

2. If he proves by his own oath, or another's testimony, that he did not take a voucher when payment was made; or that the voucher then taken has been lost or destroyed, he may be allowed any item the payment of which is satisfactorily proved by the testimony of the person to whom he made it; or if that person be dead or cannot after diligent search be found, by any competent evidence, other than his own oath, unless the surrogate is satisfied that the charge is correct and just.

The payments to be made by an executor may be for the following purposes:

1. Funeral expenses.
2. Expenses of administration of the corpus of the estate.
3. Expenses attending income arising out of the estate.

4. Payments of decedent's debts.
5. Payments of legacies.
6. Payment of income to beneficiaries, if within the executor's scope of duties.
7. Payment to residuary legatees or to next of kin.

Of course no profit may be made by an executor or administrator, by the increase, nor shall he sustain any loss by the decrease without his fault, of any part of the estate; but he shall account for such increase, and be allowed for such decrease on the settlement of the account, and the surrogate may allow the accounting party for property of the decedent, perished or lost, without the fault of the accounting party.

The increase to which I have just referred will go to the increase of the assets, principal or corpus of the estate, and the decrease go to the decrease of the assets of the estate, whether the decrease be due to reduction in value on realization, or perishing or loss of assets. Yet the executor is bound to take all reasonable care of the property, and hence such assets as are subject to loss by fire should be insured, and unless it is a producing asset, the premium should be charged to the corpus of the estate; but if a producing asset, to the income which is going to beneficiaries.

We will now consider the disbursements in their order:

1. Funeral expenses. So long as these are reasonable, and becoming the condition of the estate of decedent, they will be allowed and are chargeable to corpus of the estate.

2. Expenses of administration, except such as are directly consumed with income, are chargeable to corpus of estate.

3. Expenses concerned with income are to be taken out of income.

4. Payment of decedent's debts. In payment of these two things have to be noticed:—

A. Ascertainment of debts.

B. Order of payments.

1. Ascertainment of debts. The executor or administrator, at any time after the granting of the letters, may insert a notice, once each week for six months, in such newspaper or newspapers printed in the county as the surrogate directs, requiring all persons having claims against the deceased to exhibit the same, with the vouchers therefor, to him at a place to be speci-

fied in the notice, at or before a day therein named, which must be at least six months from the day of the first publication of the notice. The executor or administrator may require satisfactory vouchers in support of any claim presented, and the affidavit of the claimant that the claim is justly due, that no payments have been made thereon and that there are no offsets against the same to the knowledge of the claimant. If a suit be brought on a claim which is not presented to the executor or administrator within six months from the first publication of such notice, the executor or administrator shall not be chargeable for any assets or moneys that he may have paid in satisfaction of any lawful claims or of any legacies, or in making distribution to the next of kin before such suit was commenced.

2. The order of payments :—

Every executor and administrator must proceed with diligence to pay the debts of the deceased, according to the following order:

1. Debts entitled to a preference under the laws of the United States. Since the repeal of the inheritance law the only important one is the bond given to pay duties.

2. Taxes assessed on the property of the deceased during his lifetime; but taxes assessed on real estate subsequent to his death are not to be paid by an executor or administrator as such. It belongs to the testamentary trustee to pay them. Hence there may arise a question when they are assessed. In New York City, the time seems to be when the books are delivered into the hands of the receiver of taxes for collection.

3. Judgments docketed and decisions entered against the deceased according to the priority thereof respectively.

4. All recognizances, bonds, sealed instruments, notes, bills and unliquidated demands and accounts.

Each class is entitled to payment in full before any payments can be made upon a debt of a subsequent class.

Preference shall not be given in the payment of a debt over other debts of the same class, except those specified in the third class. A debt due and payable shall not be entitled to a preference over debts not due; nor shall the commencement of a suit for the recovery of a debt, or the obtaining of a judgment thereon remove the debt from class four (4) to class three (3).

Debts not due may be paid, according to the class to which they belong, after deducting a rebate of legal interest on sum paid for the unexpired term of credit. An executor or administrator shall not satisfy his own debt or claim out of the property of the deceased, until proved to, or allowed by, the surrogate; and it shall not have the preference over others of the same class. Preference may be given by the surrogate to rents due or accruing on leases held by the testator or intestate at the time of his death over debts of the fourth class, if it appears to his satisfaction that such preference will benefit the estate of the testator or intestate.

Rents, annuities and dividends shall, on the death, or other sooner determination of the beneficiary therein, be apportioned so that he or his executors, administrators or assigns, shall be entitled to a proportion of such rents, annuities, dividends, or other payments of like nature, according to the time which shall have elapsed from the commencement or last period of payment thereof, as the case may be, including the day of the death of such person or of the determination of his interest, after making allowance and deductions on account of charges on such rents, annuities, dividends and other payments. Every such person or his executors, administrators or assigns shall have the same remedies at law and in equity for recovering such apportioned parts of such rents, annuities, dividends or other payments, when the entire amount of which such apportioned parts form part, become due and payable, and not before, as he or they would have had for recovering and obtaining such entire rents, annuities, dividends and other payments, if entitled thereto; but the persons liable to pay rents reserved by any lease or demise, or the real property comprised therein, shall not be resorted to for such apportioned part, but the entire rents of which such apportioned parts form parts must be collected and recovered by the person or persons who but for this section would have been entitled to the entire rents; and such portions shall be recoverable from such person or persons by the parties entitled to the same.

An assessment confirmed at the time of testator's decease, although a lien upon the real estate, is also a debt to be paid out of the personal estate, but in the fourth class.

Foreign judgments do not belong to the third class, but to the fourth class.

Mortgages cannot be paid out of the personal estate, unless so provided by will, in which case they belong to the fourth class.

Where a creditor has additional security, he should first exhaust that security and only have recourse to the personal property for deficiency.

Creditors of an insolvent partnership, in case of the death of one of the partners, cannot collect their debts against the separate estate of the decedent until his individual liabilities shall have been paid in full.

A voluntary bond of the testator given in his lifetime, payable at or immediately after his death, is a valid debt, and has preference over legacies, but is postponed to debts for valuable considerations.

The executor or administrator will not be protected in paying a debt or claim barred by the statute of limitations, nor will his promise revive such a claim.

To this point the law is supreme; after this point the will is efficacious.

LECTURE VII.

LEGACIES, AND A SUMMARY OF THE PRINCIPLES OF ACCOUNTING.

No legacy shall be paid by an executor or administrator until after the expiration of one year from the time of granting letters testamentary or of administration, unless directed by the will to be sooner paid. If directed to be sooner paid, the executor or administrator may require a bond, with two sufficient securities, on condition that if the debts against deceased duly appear, and there are not other assets sufficient to pay other legacies, then the legatees will refund the legacy so paid or such ratable portion thereof with the other legatees, as may be necessary for the payment of such debts, and the proportionable parts of such legacies, if there be any, and the costs and charges incurred by reason of the payment to such legatee; and that if the probate of the will under which such legacy is paid be revoked, or the will be declared void, such legatee will refund the whole of such legacy, with interest, to the executor or administrator entitled thereto.

After the expiration of one year the executors or administrators must discharge the specific legacies bequeathed by the will and pay the general legacies if there be assets. If these be not sufficient, then an abatement of the general legacies must be made in equal proportions. Such payment shall be enforced by the surrogate in the same manner as the return of an inventory and by a suit on the bond of such executor or administrator, whenever directed by the surrogate.

A legacy is a gift of personalty by will. It may be :—

1. A general legacy (pecuniary), one payable out of the general assets of the testator.

2. A specific legacy, a bequest of a specific part of the personalty.

3. A demonstrative legacy, partaking of the nature of a specific legacy; when the fund or portion of the estate is designated as the source from which payment is to be made, so far it is specific; but in not pointing out the specific portion of the fund it is general.

Another division of legacies is :—

1. Vested, when the right of the property therein is acquired, notwithstanding the deferment of the enjoyment of the same.

2. Contingent, which depend on the fulfillment of some contingency or survivorship.

Another division is into absolute and conditional.

All classes of legacies may lapse by failure of a person to take them, or be adeemed by the destruction of the subject matter in the lifetime of the testator.

If a legatee predecease the testator, the intended legacy lapses and falls into the residue of the estate; but if the legatee be a child or other issue of the testator and predecease the testator, leaving issue living at the time of the death of the testator, then such intended legacy shall not lapse, but shall take effect as if the death of such intended legatee had happened immediately after the death of the testator.

We will now proceed to the accounting, gathered from the law as already given. The will gives the executor or testamentary trustee the title to the property, which must be confirmed by the court. Under this the executor or trustee may act to a limited extent in preserving the property and in distributing the corpus, prior to qualification.

Having qualified, it gives him the ownership so far as concerns the power of collecting the assets and suing for them.

Next an inventory is made of the personal property, with estimated values of it taken by appraisers. Now begins accounting. The executor, as trustee, holds the property for the benefit of creditors and those interested in the accounts, with power to repel interference from them.

Under the category of duties, he debits himself with a classified set of assets, so as to show the whole of the estate in accordance with the inventory, for which he is answerable. The total of the inventory is the estimated value of the estate. Any one of the assets may be increased at the expense of another and his relation to those creditors and those interested may not be altered, for the sum total of the assets will remain the same and the interest of no one will be affected. There is a mere shifting of values. Any newly discovered property must be inventoried, and the executor must debit himself with the value of the discovery. If on realization of an asset by sale the value of the estate is increased, he must debit himself with the increase; for this is considered a profit, and all profits from sales go to the estate. If in the realization the value of the estate is decreased, he must credit himself with the decrease. Total of executor's indebtedness = value of original entry + value of additional inventories + increase of values of assets over and above inventoried values.

An executor may have been indebted to the decedent at the time of the decedent's death; he cannot hold his indebtedness as an offset to a legacy, or a legacy as an offset to the indebtedness, for in the event of the amount distributable to the legatees being insufficient to pay them in full, as a debtor to the estate he is held in full, but as a legatee he receives only his scaled legacy, like other legatees.

It is a general principle in trustees' accounting that the trustee can receive no benefit from an estate, except such as is given him under a will or as commission for his services, and that he is supposed to do all work connected with the estate, for which he will receive no pay, but that the surrogate may allow him for services of others, if they are necessary, and grant him extra compensation if his services are extraordinary. This condition puts it out of the power of the trustee to make and legally enforce extra compensation. The surrogate, the legal substitute of the deceased, is allowed to decide. The will may override all this.

The assets with which the executor by virtue of his office has debited himself, must in the nature of things remain assets; they cannot possibly pass into liabilities. Yet he may enter into another relation by properly disposing of them, in which case he becomes a creditor in the language of the law with respect to them. If he can account for any portion of them passing lawfully out of his hands, he is credited with that portion, and this he may have to do at an intermediate accounting, showing what remains, with which he is still debited.

He will be credited with all administrative expenses, with all losses which have arisen through no fault of his own, with all payments to creditors and legatees, so long as the distribution is according to law, and with a residue if there be one, making the sum of his credits equal the sum of his debits.

This equation is the foundation of the system. The sum of the executor's debits equals the sum of his credits; i. e., whatever came into his hands has been legally passed out. The bookkeeping as laid down by the law is one of single entry; not the single entry of commercial bookkeeping, which is founded on proprietorship, but of bookkeeping founded on trusteeship.

LECTURE VIII.

ORDER OF DISTRIBUTION OF RESIDUE—ADVANCEMENTS, COMMISSIONS.

If the deceased died intestate, the surplus of his personal property after payment of debts, and if he left a will, such surplus, after the payment of debts and legacies, if not bequeathed, must be distributed to his widow, children or next of kin, in the manner following:

1. One-third part to the widow, and the residue in equal portions among the children, and such persons as legally represent the children, if any of them have died before the deceased.

2. If there be no children, nor any legal representatives of them, then one-half of the whole surplus shall be allotted to the widow, and the other half distributed to the next of kin of the deceased entitled thereto.

3.   If the deceased leaves a widow, and no descendant, parents, brother or sister, nephew or niece, then the widow shall be entitled to the whole surplus; but if there be a brother or sister, nephew or niecé, and no descendant or parent, the widow shall be entitled to one-half of the surplus, as above provided, and to the whole of the residue if it does not exceed two thousand dollars; if the residue exceeds that sum, she shall receive, in addition to the one-half, two thousand dollars; and the remainder shall be distributed to the brothers and sisters and their representatives.

4.   If there be no widow, the whole surplus shall be distributed equally among the children and such as legally represent them.

5.   If there be no widow and no children, and no representative of a child, the whole surplus shall be distributed to the next of kin, in equal degree to the deceased and their legal representatives.

6.   If the deceased leave no children, and no representatives of them, and no father, and leave a widow and a mother, the half not distributed to the widow shall be distributed in equal shares to his mother and brothers and sisters, or the representatives of such brothers and sisters; and if there be no widow, the whole surplus shall be distributed in like manner to the mother and to the brothers and sisters, or the representatives of such brothers and sisters.

7.   If the deceased leave a father and no child or descendant, the father shall take one-half, if there be a widow, and the whole, if there be no widow.

8.   If the deceased leave a mother, and no child or descendant, father, brother, sister, or representatives of a brother or sister, the mother, if there be a widow, shall take one-half; and the whole if there be no widow.

9.   If the deceased was illegitimate and leave a mother, and no child, or descendant, or widow, such mother shall take the whole, and shall be entitled to letters of administration in exclusion of all other persons. If the mother of such deceased be dead, the relatives of the deceased on the part of the mother shall take in the same manner as if the deceased had been legitimate, and be entitled to letters of administration in the same order.

10. Where the descendants or next of kin of the deceased, entitled to share in his estate, are all in equal degree to the deceased, their shares shall be equal.

11. When such descendants or next of kin are of unequal degrees of kindred, the surplus shall be apportioned among those entitled thereto according to their respective stocks, so that those who take in their own right shall receive equal shares, and those who take by representation shall receive the share to which the parent whom they represent would have been entitled if living.

12. Representation shall be admitted among collaterals in the same manner as allowed by law in reference to real estate.

13. Relatives of the half blood shall take equally with those of the whole blood in the same degree; and the representatives of such relatives shall take in like manner as the representatives of the whole blood.

14. Descendants and next of kin of the deceased, begotten before his death but born thereafter, shall take in the same manner as if they had been born in the lifetime of the deceased and had survived him.

15. If a woman die leaving illegitimate children, and no lawful issue, such children inherit her personal property as if legitimate.

On examining the above rules for distribution of residue of the personal property of an estate, we find:

1. That the widow, who is not a relative by blood, has yet in all cases special allowances made to her.

2. That taking the deceased as the central figure, and tracing the stock (stirpes) downward, he may have children; that each of them who is alive will have an equal share after providing for the widow; and the children of those who are dead will equally receive the share of the parent. This is called *per stirpes*, and not *per capita*.

3. That there being no downward stock, we proceed upward to the father, who will take the whole, except what the law gives to the widow.

4. If the downward stock of the deceased entirely fail, and the father is likewise dead, then the children of the father, or brothers and sisters of the decedent who are alive, take equal shares, and the nephews and nieces of the decedent take

the shares of their parents who are dead, share and share alike; i. e., per stirpes; but also that the widow is first provided for, and that the mother receives a share as though she were a sister.

EXAMPLES.

1. The residue of a man's personal property is $21,000; there are surviving him a widow, three children, and two grandchildren, whose parent is dead. What portion of the $21,000 will each of the survivors receive?

Answer—Widow $7,000, each of surviving children $3,500, and each of the grandchildren $1,750.

2. Show the double entry bookkeeping necessary to carry out the conditions of Question No. 1.

3. The residue of a man's personal property is $21,000. He died, leaving no children, grandchildren, or father, but he left a widow, a mother, a brother and sister alive, and two sons of a sister who predeceased him. How is the property to be distributed?

Answer—Widow $10,500, mother, brother and sister each $2,625, and each nephew $1,312.50.

ADVANCEMENTS.

If any child of a deceased person has been advanced by the deceased, by settlement or portion of real or personal property, the value thereof shall be reckoned with that part of the surplus of the personal property which remains to be distributed among the children; and if such advancement be equal or superior to the amount which according to the preceding section would be distributed to such child as his share of such surplus and advancement, such child and his descendants shall be excluded from any share in the distribution of such surplus. If such advancement be not equal to such amount, such child or his descendants shall be entitled to receive so much only as is sufficient to make all the shares of all the children in such surplus and advancement to be equal, as near as can be estimated. The maintaining or educating, or the giving of money to a child, without a view to a portion or settlement in life, shall not be deemed an advancement, nor shall the foregoing provisions of this section apply in any case where there is any real property of the intestate to descend to his heirs. Where there is a surplus of personal property to be distributed and the advancement consisted of personal property, or where a deficiency in the adjustment of an advancement of real property is chargeable on personal property, the decree for distribution, in the surrogate's court, must adjust all the advancements which have not been previously adjusted by the judgment of a court of competent jurisdiction. For that purpose, if any person to be affected by the decree is not a party to the proceeding, the surrogate must cause him to be brought in by a supplementary decree.

EXAMPLES.

1. A person dies leaving a widow and three children to share in the residue of his personal property, valued at $21,000. He has advanced during his lifetime to his eldest son $3,000, to establish him in business. What are the distributed shares of each? Widow $8,000, the eldest $2,333.34, and each of the other two $5,333.33.

2. Suppose the advancement to the eldest has been $9,000, what would each then receive? Widow $7,000, eldest nothing, the other two each $7,000.

COMMISSIONS.

Executors, administrators and testamentary trustees are entitled to commissions as given below, and it is obligatory on the surrogate to allow them. They should be apportioned among the executors, among the administrators, and among the testamentary trustees according to the services rendered by them respectively, over and above their necessary and reasonable expenses, as follows:

For receiving and paying out all sums of money not exceeding $1,000, at the rate of 5%.

For receiving and paying out any additional sums not amounting to more than $10,000, at the rate of 2½%.

For all sums above $10,000, at the rate of 1%.

If the value of the personal property amounts to $100,000 or more over all debts, each executor or administrator is entitled to the full compensation on principal and income allowed herein to a sole executor, administrator or testamentary trustee, unless there are more than three, in which case the compensation to which three would be entitled must be apportioned among them according to the services rendered by them respectively, and a like apportionment shall be made in all cases where there shall be more than one executor, administrator or testamentary trustee. Where the will provides a specific compensation to an executor or administrator, he is not entitled to any allowance for his services, unless by a written instrument filed with the surrogate he renounces the specific compensation. If a person serves under different capacities he is entitled to compensation in one capacity only, at his election.

Trustees are not required to surrender the fund on which commissions are chargeable, until the latter are paid.

Commissions must be applied in liquidation of a debt of a trustee to the estate, and in liquidation of claims against the trustee for losses resulting from negligence.

Trustees are entitled to commissions for receiving and paying out all moneys constituting the corpus of the estate, and any additions thereto from increase of any kind. Commissions can never be computed on sums exceeding the gross amount of the estate and its actual income; and the moneys paid out upon which commissions may be computed are the moneys paid out for debts and expenses of administration and to legatees or other beneficiaries which appear to diminish the estate as it exists in the hands of the trustees and to pass out of and away from the estate.

In any given trust, the commissions are computed on the amount received or paid out by all the trustees, and not on the sums received and paid out by each. Commissions are to be computed as of date of settling, not of date of filing the account, and according to the law then in force.

Commissions are allowed on annual income when the trustee is required to keep funds invested, to receive and pay out the income annually, if he does receive it, to render an account thereof to the beneficiary, and to pay over the net balance; similarly when he renders annual accounts to the court or when he is required or permitted to state his accounts with annual rests. In all these cases the commission is computed at the full rate. Computations cannot be allowed more frequently than annually. It is against the trustee's interest to allow the income to accumulate beyond a year, as in that case his commissions might be lessened.

No commission is allowed on specific legacies. An annuity, which is a series of legacies, like a legacy is not chargeable with commissions, but where a beneficiary receives the use of a fund, the beneficiary is to be charged with commission. In all these cases, commissions on income are computed on each occasion at the full rate; viz., on the first thousand dollars, 2½% for receipts and 2½% for payments, etc. The total amount of income for the year must be taken as the basis.

EXAMPLES.

1. Two trustees collect income for one year for the use of a beneficiary, amounting to $20,000; the expense attending the same amounts to $2,000. With what sum shall the beneficiary be charged for commission, and how much for equal services should each trustee receive on the annual accounting, also how much will be due the beneficiary?

Total commission $390, each trustee's commission $195, and amount due beneficiary $18,610.

2. Four trustees receive and pay out of the corpus of an estate $200,000; the debts amount to $50,000. Supposing that their services are equal, what should each trustee receive for commission? Answer—$1,567.50.

3. Executor A receives of corpus of an estate $20,000, and Executor B receives $30,000; they pay out together $40,000. What will be the amount going to the residuary legatees? What will be the commission of each executor, their services being reckoned in proportion to the amount each executor received? A's commission $276, B's $414. Residuary legatees would receive $9,310.

LECTURE IX.

INVESTMENTS AND REALIZATION OF PROPERTY.

The trustee should at all times keep the trust fund fully in-invested, and if he neglects to invest within a reasonable time he may personally be charged with interest for the unreasonable time. He is accountable for all interest actually received arising out of the trust fund, and for all which he might have obtained by due diligence and exercise of ordinary ability.

The property being once well invested, the investments should not be changed without good reason; e. g., if the investment has become insecure the estate might suffer loss; or if it has become unproductive, the beneficiary may be suffering in income. The trustee should not traffic in trust securities, as he thereby endangers the fund, yet if a security has acquired a speculative value much above its par as an investment, the investment should be changed so that the life beneficiary may receive the increase of income to which he is entitled. The two objects which the trustee should have in view are: first, security, to protect the interest of the remainderman; and productiveness, so that the life beneficiary may receive the current rate of interest.

A testator sometimes provides that his business shall be carried on after his death for a certain time. In such a case it is the trustee's duty so to do, but if the matter is permissive, he should not continue it against his own judgment.

A partnership cannot be continued after a change in the firm, nor should the capital be increased. A trustee should never be tempted to hazard the safety of the fund so as to make unusually large returns.   .

The following may be pointed out as unfit investments: Loans on merely personal security, investments on unincorporated business ventures, partnerships, patents, second mortgages, and mortgages on leasehold property, unproductive real estate and all investments of an untried or speculative nature.

INVESTMENT OF TRUST FUNDS IN STATE OF NEW YORK.

Section 9, Chapter 295. Laws of 1902. "An executor, administrator, guardian, trustee or other person holding trust funds for investment may invest the same in the same kind of securities as those in which savings banks of this state are by law authorized to invest the money deposited therein and the income derived therefrom; and in bonds and mortgages on unincumbered real property in this state worth fifty per cent. more than the amount loaned thereon."

Sec. 116. Banking Law of 1902. "In the stocks or bonds oi interest bearing obligations of the United States, or those for which the United States are pledged to provide for the payment of the interest and principal, including the bonds of the District of Columbia.

"In the stocks or bonds or interest bearing obligations of this state, issued pursuant to the authority of any law of the state."

"In the stocks or bonds or interest bearing obligations of any state of the United States which has not within ten years previous to making such investment by such corporation defaulted in the payment of any part of either principal or interest of any debt authorized by the legislature of any such state to be contracted; and in the bonds or interest bearing obligations of any state of the United States, issued in pursuance of the authority of the legislature of such state, which have prior to the passage of this act been issued for the funding or settlement of any previous obligation of such state theretobefore in default and on which said funding or settlement obligation there has been no default in the payment of either principal or interest, since the issuance of such funded or settlement obligation, and provided the interest on such funded or settlement obligation has been paid regularly for a period not less than ten years next preceding such investments.

"In the stocks or bonds of any city, county, town or village, school district bonds, and union free school district bonds issued for school purposes, or in the interest-bearing obligations of any city or county of this state, issued pursuant to the authority of any law of the state for the payment of which the faith and credit of the municipality issuing them are pledged.

"In the stocks and bonds of the following cities: Boston, Worcester, Cambridge, Lowell, Fall River, Springfield, and Holyoke, in the State of Massachusetts; St. Louis, in the State of Missouri; Cleveland, Cincinnati and Toledo, in the State of Ohio; Detroit and Grand Rapids, in the State of Michigan; Providence, in the State of Rhode Island; New Haven and Hartford, in the State of Connecticut; Portland, in the State of

Maine; Philadelphia, Pittsburg, Allegheny, Reading and Scranton, in the State of Pennsylvania; Minneapolis and St. Paul, in the State of Minnesota; Des Moines, in the State of Iowa; Milwaukee, in the State of Wisconsin; Louisville, in the State of Kentucky; Paterson, Trenton, Newark and Camden, in the State of New Jersey; Baltimore, in the State of Maryland; Los Angeles, in the State of California. If at any time the indebtedness of any of said cities, less its water debt and sinking fund, shall receive seven per centum of its valuation for the purposes of taxation, its bonds and stocks shall thereafter, and until such indebtedness shall be reduced to seven per centum of the valuation for the purposes of taxation, cease to be an authorized investment for the money of savings banks."

Also in the securities of certain railroads, for which see Banking Law as amended by the legislature, 1902.

REALIZATION OF PROPERTY.

Certain property may not come into the hands of the trustee immediately on the assumption of the trust, so that the life beneficiary will be deprived of any benefit from it. When this fund is realized it must be so apportioned that the life beneficiary will receive income from it at the usual rate of interest from the beginning of the trust and the balance of the fund will go to the corpus. The interest on the portion going to the corpus, from the beginning of the trust to the realization, at the usual rate added to the corpus will give the amount realized. The interest should be compounded from year to year.

EXAMPLE.

A sum of money, the payment of which is deferred two years after the beginning of the trust, is then received, amounting to $10,000 with interest at the rate of 6% per annum. How will the fund be apportioned between corpus and income? Solution: One dollar at compound interest in two years will amount to $1.1236 and $10,000 divided by $1.1236 gives $8,-899.96 for the corpus and $1,100.04 for income.

If the sum of money was entered in the inventory at $8,-899.96, then on receipt of the amount cash would be debited

$10,000, and the inventory value would be credited $8,899.96 and the income credited $1,100.04. If the inventoried value should be $9,000, then there would be a loss of $100.04 with which personal estate account is debited and the realized account credited.

Illustrations. A legacy receivable not immediately received. A sum not received in full. An unsuitable investment sold and converted into a suitable one.

Unproductive property. Converted by sale into productive. Property converted because the earnings are greatly in excess of usual interest as in case of business or partnership or on wasting investments.

CORPUS AND INCOME DISTINGUISHED.

The instrument creating the trust decides conclusively what shall go to the life tenant and what to the remainderman. It is simply a question as to the intention of the creator of the trust. If the trust instrument is silent as to the apportioning of corpus and income, the general rules prevail.

1. If a mortgage held in trust is foreclosed and the land is bought in by one of the trustees, and later sold at an advance, the proceeds, over and above interest on the debt, go to capital (5 Dem. 73).

2. If trust property is destroyed by fire, the insurance money belongs to the corpus (4 Dem. 404), unless the beneficiary has paid the insurance premium.

3. A bond which forms part of the property settled on the trustee should be inventoried at par, and if sold the profit on the sale goes to the corpus, but the beneficiary receives the whole of the coupon interest, and as interest is reckoned from day to day, *pro rata* of the interest uncollected to the date of sale (103 N. Y. 445).

If, however, the bonds are purchased at a premium by the trustee, then the nominal interest is apportioned between interest and principal, the former going to the income and the latter forming a sinking fund to meet the premium of the bond when the bond matures. In this latter case the rate per cent. the bond is yielding is found from a bond table, such as Price's, etc.

EXAMPLE.

A bond per $100, nominal rate 4%, has 2 years to run, is bought for $101.93, yielding the trustee 3% interest, payable semi-annually. Show the steps in the account keeping.

Debit the bond account and credit the cash account at purchase $101.93. Half yearly interest at 3% on $101.93 is $1.53, which taken from coupon $2 gives $.47 for sinking fund.

Now debit cash $2 for coupon received and credit income $1.53 for interest, and credit the bond account with $.47, the amount required to sink premium, leaving the value of the bond $101.93—$.47=$101.46. Next the half yearly interest at 3% per annum on $101.46 is $1.52, which taken from the coupon $2 gives $.48 for the sinking fund. Debit cash $2 for coupon received and credit income $1.52 for interest, and the bond account $.48 for the sinking fund.

Proceed in this way to the end of the 2 years, and the result will be exactly $100. Now debit cash $100 for the redemption of the bond and credit the bond account with the same. It will be noticed that the premium has been returned into the cash ready for reinvestment, as also the interest ready for distribution to the beneficiaries.

4. Dividends. The general rule is that dividends belong to him who holds the stock when the dividend is declared and allotted, irrespective of when the earnings accrued or when the dividend is payable. Consequently a dividend earned before a testator's death, but declared and paid after, goes to income. This rule applies as between a life beneficiary and a remainderman, but interest accruing *de die in diem* is apportionable, e. g., in the case of interest on a mortagage. The courts have held that the same rule applies, whether the dividend is paid in cash, scrip or stock.

If there is a mere *pro rata* distribution of treasury stock to the stockholders, not representing profits, it belongs to the corpus and not to the income. Its issue decreases to that extent the value of the original shares, giving to the stockholders a larger number of shares, but no larger fund, and the total issue represents capital only.

Privileges or option given to stockholders to subscribe for stock and bonds, which option has a value of its own, is held by the trustees as capital, not income.

If a corporation is consolidated with another, and for the purpose of equalizing the interest of shareholders of the stock in question, there is during the life tenancy an extra issue to them of stock or of bonds of the consolidated company, this surplus issue merely follows the interest which it is issued to equalize.

In allotting stock dividends to life tenants, only such portion should be distributed as represents earnings; e. g., if stock has been bought at a premium, and an extraordinary dividend has been declared, it must be ascertained whether the selling price of the stock remains as high as that at which it was bought, and if it has fallen the difference must be taken from the extraordinary dividend, and accounted as corpus, and the balance of the dividend will be income.

Contracts of trust. Contracts entered into by decedent prior to his death must be carried out by trustees, and any profits resulting therefrom will belong to the corpus and not to income.

Receiving payment on account. It is held in the matter of Tietgen (5 Dem. 350) that payments paid on account of a debt, though not exceeding the accrued interest, must be considered as capital, not income. Should the entire debt be paid, with interest, the interest would constitute income.

LECTURE X.

GENERAL REMARKS ON OFFSETS TO INCOME AND TO CORPUS; ALSO ON APPORTIONMENT AND ADJUSTMENTS OF EXPENDITURES BETWEEN CORPUS AND INCOME.

1. The intent of the trust instrument must be followed in making deductions from (i. e., charges against) income.

2. The creator of the trust may order corpus as well as income to be paid to the beneficiary.

3. He may direct income to be paid subject to charges which ordinarily belong to corpus.

4. The income may be granted subject to an annuity of a certain amount.

5. He may order the gross income to be paid to the beneficiary.

But where not in opposition to the trust, the following are the principal rules in relation to the above offsets, apportionment and adjustments:

1. Taxes and assessments which have become a debt of the testator prior to his decease are payable by the executor out of corpus.

2. Expenses incurred in the borrowing of money to invest in government bonds, so as to avoid the tax otherwise payable out of income, are chargeable against income.

3. Trustees' commissions on rent and income come out of income.

4. Trustees' commissions for receiving and paying out corpus come out of corpus.

5. Fees for legal expenses in litigation resulting in a trustee's appointment in place of a predecessor removed come out of corpus.

6. Ordinary repairs must be charged against income, otherwise the corpus will be depleted for the benefit of income.

7. Interest on incumbrances, e. g., on mortgages, must be borne by the beneficiary, i. e., taken out of income.

8. The sundry expenses in conducting a business, such as wages, rent, loss from bad debts, and depreciation of plant, come out of income.

In apportionment and adjustment the following cases require to be considered:

1. Expenditures required to be made on property received by trustee in an unfructiferous condition, in order to preserve it from decay, constitute a mere shifting of the fund.

2. Where the trustee under the trust is authorized to invest and reinvest in real estate, he may make improvements on the theory that such expenditure constitutes an investment. This also is a mere shifting of the fund.

3. Where the expenditure is essential to preserve the estates from destruction, and results in a benefit both to the beneficiary and the remainderman.

4. Where the expenditure is required to make the estates

produce revenue, or a substantial revenue, and also to en-
hance the value of property, there is a mere shifting of the
fund.

5. Where there are wasting values, it is necessary to charge
the income with a sinking fund in order to preserve the corpus.

6. Compulsory outlays, such as municipal assessments for
flagging sidewalks, widening streets, repairs or reconstruction
ordered by building department, must be so charged as to affect
equitably the beneficiary and the remainderman, and this may
or may not be by apportionment of the outlay, according to
the requirements of the case.

EXAMPLES.

1. Peck vs. Sherwood, 56 N. Y., 615. Here the life interest
in land is vested in one person, and the remainder vested in
another, and there is no fund in which the two have an interest
in common, but there is an available fund in the hands of the
trustee in which the life tenant has no interest. The trustee of
the remainderman was authorized by the court to unite with
the life tenant in an outlay to protect the property in which the
remainderman and the life tenant have interests in common.
The capital was charged one portion exclusively out of the
available fund, in which the life tenant had no interest; leaving the other portion exclusively as a liability against the life
tenant. The interest of the life tenant in the real estate is
found by Northampton tables, and this taken from the total
value of the real estate affected gives the interest of the remainderman.

The apportionment of the outlay must be in proportion to
these respective interests, hence as the total value of the
real estate is to life tenant's interest, so is the total outlay to
life tenant's share of outlay.

2. Stevens vs. Melcher, 80 Hun. 514 (522-525) is a more
common case. Here the trustee held in trust both real and
personal property, in which the remainderman and the life
tenant had interests in common. For an outlay on the real
estate, the adjustment of interests was made by charging the
whole of the outlay against capital, i. e., the whole was taken
out of capital (corpus), thus bringing about an automatic ad-

justment by the remainderman losing the amount of the outlay and the life tenant the income from the portion lost.

The same applies in Whittemore vs. Beekman, 2 Dem. 275 (283), where a loss is sustained in an authorized investment; also in another branch of the Stevens vs. Melcher case (80 Hun., 525 *seq.*), where the outlay has effected a corresponding increase in the value of the improved real estate; a charge of the outlay to the extent of the entire permanent increase may be taken out of capital, as by this means there is a mere shifting of investment from personalty to realty, while any balance over and above permanent increase may be charged directly to income.

3. In Cogswell vs. Cogswell, 2 Edw. Ch. 231 (240-242), certain buildings in Cedar Street are left in trust with remainder. The city in widening the street cut off ten feet in front. The court directed that the cost of erecting warehouses on the lots be paid from the available capital; that out of the rents 6% of the cost of the buildings be reserved, together with a reasonable allowance for depreciation of the buildings until the life estates fall. In this case the life tenants receive the net receipts and profits of this portion of the estate, and in the meantime the money expended is a good and safe investment, drawing 6% during the life estate.

In the case of only one life tenant the expectation-of-life table will give the average of life for the life tenant. Then the difference between the estimated value of the buildings at the end of the average life and the present value will give the total depreciation, which, divided by the average life, will give the depreciation to be written off yearly from the income as a sinking fund to the cost.

4. In Swain vs. Perine, 5 Johns Ch. 482 (491 *seq.*), a widow filed a bill for assignment of dower and mesne profits; the heirs had been obliged to pay off a mortgage to which the dower interest was subject. The decree gave the widow one-third and mesne profits, less her ratable contribution toward the redemption of the mortgage. The court held that in view of her getting her third from the mortgage she ought to pay interest on one-third of the mortgage debt paid by the heirs, but as this method would be inconvenient and embarrassing, the direction was that the value of such annual payment

for her life should be computed and subtracted from the mesne profits*, any excess to be subtracted from the dower assigned.

5. Stillwell vs. Doughty, 2 Bradf. 311. Where there was no trust a sewer assessment was wholly charged on the remainderman, and the life tenant was directed to pay interest on the assessment.

When property does not immediately pass into the hands of the trustee at the beginning of the trust, such a sum of money, called the present worth, must be found as at the current rate of interest for the time between the beginning of the trust and the time it passes into the trustee's hands will amount to the value passing into his hands. This present worth is corpus, and the difference between it and the amount passing into his hands is income.

· EXAMPLES.

1. The amount of legacy not immediately received.

2. Where the property, being an unsuitable investment, is sold for conversion some time after the beginning of the trust.

3. Where the property is converted because of its unproductiveness ; such as vacant lots.

4. Where principal and interest payable during trust are contained in one sum.

5. On an obligation in which the whole cannot be collected in the realization.

6. Gain or loss in temporarily conducting a business until it is converted.

Wasting property, which may be of several kinds:

1. Where the waste is indeterminate, until it is suddenly discovered as in the case of a mining property, or in a mining stock.

The best way to treat this is to give the life tenant a current rate of interest on the inventory value, out of the gross income received, and to carry the balance to reduce the inventory. The current rate is to be continued on the diminishing value so long as there remains any balance. If after the capi-

---

* The mesne profits are the profits of land while in the possession of a person not the owner.

tal has been wiped out income should be received, it will form corpus going to the remainderman. Of course, this new corpus should be reinvested so as to yield further income.

Where the gross income is certain and the waste is determinate, but to the extent of only a part of the property: This is the case with a bond purchased by a trustee above par, the waste part being the premium. The rate per cent. the bond is actually yielding is to be determined from bond tables, and from the value of the bond and rate per cent. it yields can be found the interest, which taken from the coupons received gives what is usually called the sinking fund. The income account is debited with the sinking fund and the bond account credited. The bond account is thus reduced in value by the operation, and the process is continued, using each time the diminishing balance, instead of the inventory value, until the premium is wiped out. The same method is applicable to an annuity receivable by estate, except that the process is continued until the annuity is extinguished.

3. In the case of a lease to the decedent during his lifetime, in which there is a yearly gain over rent to owner, repairs, insurance, etc., which has a term of years yet unexpired, the following is the *modus operandi* for keeping the accounts:

We presume that there is an account among the assets, representing the inventory value of the lease, which we will call *lease account*. On receiving and disbursing for account of this lease open another account called *realization of lease account*. Debit cash yearly with all income and credit the realization account with the same. Also debit realization account yearly with all disbursements and credit cash with the same. Two cases may present themselves:

(a) The credits may exceed the debits, and the difference will give the net realization, which is made up of both corpus and income received for the year, and which require to be separated.

(b) The debits may exceed the credits, and the difference contains neither corpus nor income, but simply a diminution of corpus for the year.

If the second case obtains, debit personal estate account with diminution of corpus and credit realization account with the same.

To separate the corpus from the income requires:

1. Choosing a rate per cent. of interest which should be such as can be obtained in investments of a safe kind.

2. A table of present values at the given rate per cent. of $1, payment of which is deferred, for one, two, three years, etc.

If there be a net realization at the end of the first year, then multiply the net realization at end of first year by the present value of $1, payment of which is deferred one year at the said rate per cent. If there be a net realization at the end of, say, the third year, then multiply net realization by the present value of $1, payment of which is deferred three years, etc., etc., to obtain the corpus which is then realized. Having obtained it, debit the realization account with it, and credit the lease account with the same.

At the end of any period debit realization account with net income and credit income account with same. Finally balance the lease account into the personal estate account for increase or decrease of realization over inventory value, when there is an income.

From observing the entries carried into the personal estate account it will be seen how much the inventory value of lease was overvalued or undervalued.

Apportionment of rents, annuities and dividends. These relate to sums of money regularly payable or becoming due.

If an estate merely devolves on another as from a decedent to an heir, or to a life beneficiary, or from an executor to a trustee, the estate is not determined, and there is no apportionment; but if an estate is determined by the death of a recipient of the rents, annuities and dividends, then there is an apportionment reckoned from the last payment to the evening of the death of the last recipient. It, however, is only recoverable when the entire amount of which such apportionment forms part becomes due and payable and not before, from the person entitled to collect the whole.

Edward Brown's Estate

1	Debtors to Estate:—
1	Henry Edmonson
2	William Smith
3	Henry Smithson
4	John May
5	Henry Smith
6	Legacy left to decedent, but not paid him
2	Creditors of Estate:—
1	William Hopetown
2	Henry Thompson
3	Henry Arnold
4	Judgment Creditors
3	Sundry expenses:—
1	Funeral expenses
2	Probate expenses
3	Transfer tax on Legacy left decedent
4	Accountant's and Attorney's fees
5	Commission, i. e., Legacy left in lieu of commission
4	Sundry persons interested in Estate:—
1	Elizabeth Brown, widow of decedent, life beneficiary of proceeds of mortgage
2	John Brown, son of decedent, residuary legatee
3	John Brown, next of kin of Elizabeth Brown

CLASSIFICATION OF ACCOUNTS

1	Personal Estate account
2	Asset accounts
3	Distributive accounts

Accounts and Transactions of Henry Arlington, Executor

1	1900 Dec.	1	Edward Brown died this day, having nominated H. Arlington Executor				
2		1	Inventory taken and appraised				
			Mortgages receivable	8,000			
			Furniture	1,000			
			Cash in house	800			
			Debts due deceased, Henry Edmonson	1,000			
			Wm. Smith	500			
			Henry Smithson	500			
			John May	250			
			Accrued interest on mortgage for 5 months to date	166	67	12,216	67
3	Dec.	31	Found that decedent owes State Transfer tax on legacy left him, being at 5 per cent. on $1,000	50			
4		31	Collected 6 months' interest ($8,000 at 5 per cent.) to date	200			
5	1901 Feb.	1	Newly discovered assets:— Henry Smith's indebtedness to decedent	200			
			Legacy left by Millard Werner, deceased	1,000			
6			Received above legacy	1,000			
7		2	Approved the following claims against Estate:—				
			Funeral expenses	150			
			Probate expenses	100			
			William Hopetown, amount of his bill	50			
			Henry Thomson, amount of his bill	40			
			Henry Arnold, amount of his bill	10			
8		2	Paid the following :—				
			Tax on legacy	50			
			Funeral expenses	150			
			Probate expenses	100			
			William Hopetown	50			
			Henry Thomson	40			
			Henry Arnold	10			
			Life beneficiary	140			
9	June	30	Received 6 months' interest on mortgage to date	200			
			Received amount of mortgage paid off this day	8,000			
			Henry Edmonson paid his indebtedness to Estate	1,000			
			William Smith paid his indebtedness to Estate	500			
			Henry Smithson paid on account	200			
			Furniture sold by auction this day	800			
10			Depreciation on sale of furniture	200			
11	July	1	Deposited in Knickerbocker Trust Co.	10,000			

JOURNAL

————————1st December, 1900————————				12,216	67
Sundries to Personal Estate account					
Mortgages receivable	8,000				
Furniture	1,000				
Cash in house	800				
Debts due decedent :—					
Henry Edmonson	1,000				
William Smith	500				
Henry Smithson	500				
John May	250				
Interest accrued on mortgage for 5 months to date	166	67			
As per inventory taken this day					
————————31st December, 1900————————					
Personal Estate account	50				
To Legacy account				50	
For amount of transfer tax on legacy to deceased					
———————— 1st February, 1901————————					
Sundries to Personal Estate account				1,200	
For newly discovered assets					
Henry Smith, indebtedness to Estate	200				
Legacy from Estate of Millard Werner	1,000				
————————2nd February, 1901————————					
Personal Estate to Sundries	350				
Funeral expenses				150	
Probate expenses				100	
Wm. Hopetown, amount of his bill				50	
Henry Thomson, amount of his bill				40	
Henry Arnold, amount of his bill				10	
———————— 30th June, 1901————————					
Personal Estate account	200				
To Furniture account				200	
For depreciation on sale of furniture					

IN ACCORDANCE WITH DECREE OF SURROGATE, IT WILL BE NECESSARY TO MAKE THE FOLLOWING ENTRIES:

Personal Estate account to Cash		700		700
To pay judgment creditors				
Personal Estate account to Cash		1,000		1,000
For commission	500			
For Accountant's and Attorney's fee	500			
Life beneficiary account to Cash		60		60
For amount paid John Brown as next of kin				
Personal Estate account to Sundries		11,150		
Cash				400
Knickerbocker Trust Co.				10,000
H. Smithson's account (Assignment)				500
Jno. May's account (Assignment)				250
For assets turned over to John Brown as residuary legatee				
The above entries have been posted to their respective accounts as of 1st July, 1901, in order to close accounts of the Ledger				

DR. CASH BOOK AND CASH ACCOUNT OF ESTATE OF EDWARD BROWN.

1900					
Dec.	1	Cash in house as per inventory		800	
	31	Interest accrued account—Interest to 1st inst. 166.67			
		Life beneficiary account—Interest from 1st inst. to date 33.33		200	
1901					
June	1	Legacy account—Received legacy left E. Brown by the late Millard Werner		1,000	
	30	Life beneficiary account—Interest to 31st May, 1901, when life beneficiary died 166.67			
		Personal Estate account—Interest from 31st May, to date 33.33		200	
		Mortgage receivable account—Mortgage paid off this day		8,000	
		H. Edmonson paid his indebtedness		1,000	
		H. Smith paid his indebtedness		500	
		Henry Smith paid his indebtedness		200	
		Furniture account—Sold by auction this day		800	
					12,700
July	1	Balance			2,160
					2,160

CASH BOOK AND CASH ACCOUNT OF ESTATE OF EDWARD BROWN. CR.

1901					
Feb.	2	Legacy account—Paid tax on legacy		50	
		Funeral expenses account—Undertaker's bill		150	
		Probate expenses—paid this day		100	
		William Hopetown—paid this day		50	
		Henry Thomson—paid this day		40	
		Henry Arnold—paid this day		10	
		Life beneficiary—paid her on account		140	
July	1	Knickerbocker Trust Co.—deposited this date at 2 per cent.		10,000	
		Balance		2,160	
					12,700
July	1	John Brown, as widow's next of kin		60	
		Commission		500	
		Accountant's and Attorney's fees		500	
		John Brown, residuary legatee		400	
		Judgment creditors		700	
					2,160

LEDGER OF ESTATE OF EDWARD BROWN

DR.   (1) PERSONAL ESTATE ACCOUNT   CR.

1900 Dec	31	Transfer tax on legacy	50		1900 Dec.	31	Mortgages receivable	8,000	
1901 Feb.	2	Funeral expenses	150				Furniture	1,000	
		Probate expenses	100				Cash in house	800	
		William Hopetown	50				Debts due deceased		
		H. Thomson	40				Henry Edmonson	1,000	
		H. Arnold	10				William Smith	500	
June	30	Depreciation of furniture	200				Henry Smithson	500	
							John May	250	
							Accrued interest on mortgage	166	67
			600					12,216	67
July	1	Balance	12,850		1901 Feb.	1	Henry Smith for debt not included in inventory.	200	
							Legacy left by Mr. Werner.	1,000	
					June	30	Interest from 31st of May to date	33	33
			13,450					13,450	
July	1	Distributed by decree:			July	1	Balance	12,850	
		Judgment creditors	700						
		Administration expenses	1,000						
		John Brown, residuary legatee	11,150						
			12,850					12,850	

(2) MORTGAGES RECEIVABLE

| 1900 Dec. | 1 | Personal est. account | 8,000 | | 1901 June | 30 | Cash | 8,000 |

(3) FURNITURE ACCOUNT, OF WHICH THE WIDOW HAS THE USE DURING HER LIFE.

1900 Dec.	1	Personal est. account	1,000		1901 June	30	Proceeds of sale	800
							Personal est. account for loss on sale	200
			1,000					1,000

LEDGER OF ESTATE OF EDWARD BROWN

Dr.   (4) DEBTS DUE ESTATE OF EDWARD BROWN   Cr.

1900 Dec.	1	H. Edmonson	1,000		1901 June	30	H. Edmonson	1,000	
		Wm. Smith	500				Wm. Smith	500	
		Henry Smithson	500		July	1	Carried down	500	
		John May	250				" "	250	
1901 Feb.	1	Henry Smith	200		June	30	Henry Smith	200	
			2,450					2,450	
July	1	H. Smithson	500		July	1	Personal estate	500	
		Jno. May	250			1	Personal estate	250	
			750					750	

(5) INTEREST ACCRUED TO 1ST DECEMBER, 1900

| 1900 Dec. | 1 | Personal est. account | 166 | 67 | 1900 Dec. | 31 | Cash | 166 | 67 |

(6) KNICKERBOCKER TRUST CO.

| 1901 July | 1 | Cash deposited at 2 per cent. per annum | 10,000 | | 1901 July | 1 | John Brown, R. L. | 10,000 | |

(7) LEGACY RECEIVABLE ACCOUNT

1901 Feb.	1	Personal est. account	1,000		1900 Dec.	31	Personal est. account	50	
	2	Paid transfer T.	500		1901 Feb.	1	Cash	1,000	
			50						
			1,050					2,050	

————————DISTRIBUTION ACCOUNTS————————

(8) LIFE BENEFICIARY ACCOUNT (the widow died 31st May, 1900)

1901 Feb.	1	Cash on account	140		1900 Dec.	31	Interest	33	33
July	1	Balance	60		1901 June	30	Interest from 31st Dec. 1900, to 31st May, 1901	166	67
			200					200	
July	1	Jno. Brown, next of kin	60		July	1	Balance	60	

LEDGER OF ESTATE OF EDWARD BROWN

Dr.   (9)   FUNERAL EXPENSES   Cr.

1901 Feb.	2	Cash	150		1901 Feb.	2	Personal est. account	150

(10) PROBATE EXPENSES

1901 Feb.	2	Cash	100		1901 Feb.	2	Personal est. account	100

(11) DEBTS DUE BY ESTATE (Creditors).

1901 Feb.	2	Paid Wm. Hopetown " Henry Thomson " H. Arnold	50 40 10		1901 Feb.	2	Wm. Hopetown H. Thomson H. Arnold	50 40 10
			100					100

(12) TRIAL BALANCE 1ST JULY, 1901, BEFORE S. DECREE

		Cash from C. B. Henry Smithson John May Knickerbocker T. Co.	2,160 500 250 10,000				Personal est. account Est. Life Beneficiary	12,850 60
			12,910					12,910

CONTENTS OF SCHEDULES, SURROGATE COURT OF COUNTY OF NEW YORK

Amount of Inventory			12,216 67

————————————Schedule A————————————

Sales:—
    Furniture   800
Debts mentioned in Inventory, which have been collected:—
    Henry Edmonson $1,000
    William Smith   500
                                           1,500
Interest collected:—
    Total   400
    Less included in Inventory   166.67
                                           233 | 33

————————————Schedule B————————————

Debts not collected or collectible:—
    Henry Smithson   500
    John May   250
                                           750
Losses by accident   000
Assets discovered after taking of Inventory:—
    Debt due Estate by Henry Smith   200
    Legacy left deceased   1,000
                                           1,200

————————————Schedule C————————————

Expenses:—
    Untertaker's bill   150
    Probate expenses   100
    Transfer Tax on legacy   50
                                           300

————————————Schedule D————————————

Judgment Creditors:—
    Allowed   248
    Disputed   452
                                           700
Moneys paid to Creditors:—
    William Hopetown   50
    Henry Thomson   40
    Henry Arnold   10
                                           '100

————————————Schedule E————————————

All moneys paid to widow   140
All moneys paid to next kin   000,00
                                           140

————————————Schedule F————————————

Elizabeth Brown, widow of deceased, 18 St. James Place, Brooklyn
John Brown, son of deceased, 18 St. James Place, Brooklyn

————————————Schedule G————————————

H. Arlington, Executor, legacy in lieu of commission   500
    Balance due widow
Interest on mortgage from death of decedent to death of widow, viz., from 1st Dec. 1900 to 31st May   200
    1903
    Paid her on account   140
                                           60

                        LOSSES ON SALES
Appraised value of furniture   1,000
Net return of sale   800
                                           200

ACCOUNTING BEFORE SURROGATE

I, Henry Arlington, Executor, charge myself as follows:—				
With amount of inventory			12,216	67
With increase as shown in Schedules A and B				
Interest received	233	33		
Newly discovered assets	1,200		1,433	33
			13,650	
I credit myself as follows:—				
With loss on sales as per Schedule G	200			
With debts not collected, Schedule B	750			
With expenses as per Schedule C	300			
With moneys paid to creditors, Schedule D	100			
With all moneys paid to widow and next of kin, Schedule E	140		1,490	
			12,160	
Debts not collected, Schedule B			750	
Total amount to be distributed			12,910	
———————— Decree of Surrogate ————————				
Amounts coming to residuary legatee, John Brown:—				
Debts not collected	750			
Cash	400			
Knickerbocker Trust Co., deposit	10,000			
			11,150	
Amounts to be paid by Executor:—				
Due John Brown as widow's next of kin	60			
Commission allowed	500			
Accountant's and Attorney's fees	500			
Judgment creditors	700			
			1,760	
			12,910	

EXECUTOR AND TRUSTEE COMBINED, WITH ACCOUNT CARRIED TO A CERTAIN POINT

―――――――――――――ESTATE OF JOHN HOSKINS――――――――――――――

Under a Trust Deed, John Hoskins deeded to William Smith in trust his property both Real and Personal, to carry out the provisions of the Trust

Under the Trust Deed, the following are the principal provisions of the Trust:—

1. He leaves to his wife, as life beneficiary, the gross income from his personal property, and the use of his household furniture
2. He leaves to his only son, John Hoskins, all his Real Estate
3. He leaves to his only daughter, Mary, a legacy of $5,000, to be paid to her as soon as convenient after his death
4. He leaves a life insurance to Wm. Smith as Trustee, to be collected and to form part of the fund of his personal property
5. The Estate is to be carried on to the death of his wife, and the Real Estate to be transferred to the son, at the discretion of the Trustee, who is required to turn over the rents to the son as they are collected

John Hoskins died 31st March, 1899

JOURNAL

————————4th April, 1899————				
Sundries to Personal Estate account			65,769	29
Cash in Bank	250			
Household furniture	2,000			
Bank shares	45,250			
Life insurance policy	15,000			
On deposit with Trust Co., principal and interest	2,019	29		
Rent due but not paid	1,250			
As per Inventory made by appraisers this day				
————————10th April, 1899————				
Personal Estate account, Sundries	3,557	47		
For outstanding debts due by deceased, which are al-				
lowed, as there are sufficient funds to meet all demands				
Servants' wages			150	
A. Langstadter's bill			75	12
Wm. Anderson, loan from him			2,656	25
John Harris' bill			272	62
Daniel Tompson's bill			60	62
William Fife's bill			85	62
Brooks Bros.' bill			105	12
Acker, Merrill & Condit's bill			152	12
————————10th April, 1899————				
Personal Estate account to Sundries	202	50		
Funeral expenses—Undertaker's bill			150	
Dr. Sampson's bill for medical attendance			52	50
————————19th April, 1899————				
Personal Estate account	2,463	83		
To Transfer tax			2,463	83
Paid on net assets to N. Y. State				
————————13th May, 1899————				
Bank Shares account	235	62		
To life beneficiary account			235	62
For her portion of dividend (interest), from 31st				
March, 1899, to date				
————————13th May, 1899————				
Bank Shares account	289	38		
To Personal Estate account			289	38
For profit on sale of Bank shares				
————————14th May, 1899————				
Trust Co.'s account	6	12		
To life beneficiary account			6	12
For interest from 31st March, 1899, to date				
———————— 10th June, 1899————				
Personal Estate account	5,000			
To Legacy account			5,000	
For legacy left Mary Hoskins				
———————— 10th June, 1900————				
Personal Estate account	675	87		
To expenses on realization and administration			675	87
For total expenses chargeable against capital				
Commission	250			
Legal expenses	375.87			
Miscellaneous	50			

DR.   CASH BOOK AND CASH ACCOUNT OF ESTATE OF JOHN HOSKINS

1899					
April	4	Cash in Bank	250		
	18	Life insurance account—Collection of policy	15,000		
May	13	Bank shares account—Sold 400 shares at $115, less expenses of sales $225	45,775		
	14	Trust Co. account — Withdrawn deposit $2,000 with interest to date	2,025	41	
	15	Rents due but unpaid at decedent's death:—			
		Andrew Mason 375			
		Wm. J. Renall 500			
		Mary Hoskins 375			
			1,250		
		Rent account—Rent from John Hardy due since testator's death	250		
Nov.	15	Life beneficiary account—6 months' interest to date on mortgage on No. 40 W. 28th St.	1,030		
1900					
May	15	Life beneficiary account—6 months' interest to date on mortgage on No. 40 W. 28th St.	1,030		
				—	66,610	41
June	10	Balance			1,210	74

CASH BOOK AND CASH ACCOUNT OF ESTATE OF JOHN HOSKINS.   CR.

1899						
April	10	Funeral expenses	150			
		Sundry Creditors account—				
		Paid Dr. Sampson's bill	52	50		
		Servants' wages	150			
		A. Langstadter's bill	75	12		
		Wm. Anderson's loan	2,656	25		
		John Harris' bill	272	62		
		Daniel Tompson's bill	60	62		
		Wm. Fife's bill	85	62		
		Brooks Bros.' bill	105	12		
		Acker, Merrill & Condit's bill	152	12		
	19	Transfer tax paid this day	2,463	83		
May	15	Rent account—Paid John Hoskins rent received from John Hardy	250			
		Mortgage receivable account—Loan made this day secured by mortgage on No. 40 W. 28th St., N. Y.	51,500			
June	10	Legacy account—Paid Mary Hoskins her legacy	5,000			
Nov.	12	Life beneficiary account—Paid life beneficiary on account this day	750			
1900						
May	12	Life beneficiary account—Paid life beneficiary on account this day	1,000			
June	10	Expenses of realization and administration:—				
		Commission to Executor 250				
		Legal expenses 375.87				
		Miscellaneous expenses 50				
			675	87		
		Balance	1,210	74	66,610	41

LEDGER OF ESTATE OF JOHN HOSKINS

DR.   (1) PERSONAL ESTATE ACCOUNT   **CR.**

1899						1899					
Apr.	10	Servants' wages	150			Apr.	4	Cash in bank	250	
		A. Langstadter's bill	75	12				Household furniture	2,000	
		W. Anderson, loan						Bank shares	45,250	
		from him	2,656	25				Life insurancy policy	15,000	
		John Harris' bill	272	62				Trust Co., principal		
		D. Tompson's bill	60	62				and interest	2,019	29
		W. Fife's bill	85	62				Rents due but not paid	1,250	
		Brooks Brothers' bill	105	12						
		Acker, Merrill & Condit	152	12						
		Dr. Sampson's bill	52	50						
		Undertaker's bill	150							
		Balance	62,009	32						
			65,769	29					65,769	29
	19	Transfer Tax	2,463	83		Apr.	10	Balance	62,009	32
June	10	Legacy	5,000			May	13	Profit on sale of bank		
1900								shares	289	38
June	10	Commission	250							
		Legal expenses	375	87						
		Miscellaneous exp.	50							
		Balance	54,159							
			62,298	70					62,298	70
						June	10	Balance	54,159	

(2) HOUSEHOLD FURNITURE ACCOUNT

1899										
Apr.	4	Personal est. account	2,000							

(3) LIFE INSURANCE ACCOUNT

1899						1899				
Apr.	4	Personal est. account	15,000			Apr.	18	Cash	15,000	

(4) BANK SHARES ACCOUNT

1899						1899				
Apr.	4	Personal est. account	45,250			May	13	Proceeds of sale	45,775	
May	13	Dividend from 31st								
		Mch. 1899 to date	235	62						
	13	Personal est. for profit								
		on sale	289	38						
			45,775						45,775	

(5) TRUST COMPANY ACCOUNT

1899						1899				
Apr.	4	Personal est. account	2,019	29		May	14	Cash	2,025	41
May	14	Life beneficiary for in-								
		terest to date	6	12						
			2,025	41					2,025	41

LEDGER OF ESTATE OF JOHN HOSKINS

Dr.   (6) MORTGAGE RECEIVABLE ACCOUNT   Cr.

1899 May	15	Loan made this day secured by mortgage on 40 W. 28th St., New York	51,500			

(7) RENTS DUE BUT NOT PAID AT DECEDENT'S DEATH

1899 Apr.	4	Personal est. account	1,250		1899 May	15	Andrew Mason	375	
							Wm. J. Renall	500	
							Mary Hoskins	375	
			1,250					1,250	

(8) FUNERAL EXPENSES.

1899 Apr.	19	Cash	150		1899 Apr.	10	Personal est. account	150	

(9) CREDITORS OF ESTATE

1899 Apr.	19	Paid servants' wages	150		1899 Apr.	10	Servants' wages	150	
		Paid A. Langstadter	72	12			A. Langstadter's bill	75	12
		Paid W. Anderson	2,656	25			Wm. Anderson	2,656	25
		Paid J. Harris	272	62			J. Harris' bill	272	62
		Paid D. Tompson	60	62			D. Tompson's bill	60	62
		Paid W. Fife	85	62			W. Fife's bill	85	62
		Paid Brooks Bros.	105	12			Brooks Brothers' bill	105	12
		Acker, Merrill & Condit	152	12			Acker, Merrill & Condit	152	12
		Dr. Sampson's	52	50			Dr. Sampson's bill	52	50
			3,609	97				3,609	97

(10) RENT ACCOUNT

1899 May	15	Paid J. Hoskins, son of decedent, rent received	250		1899 May	15	Rec'd from Jno. Hardy rent due since testator's death	250	

(11) LEGACY ACCOUNT

1899 June	10	Cash	5,000		1899 June	10	Personal est. account	5,000	

LEDGER OF ESTATE OF JOHN HOSKINS

DR. (12) LIFE BENEFICIARY ACCOUNT (Died 14th May, 1900) CR.

1899						1899				
Nov.	12	Pd L. B. on account	750			May	13	Interest on B. S. to date	235	62
1900							14	Interest from Trust Co.	6	12
May	12	Pd L. B. on account	1,000			Nov.	15	6 mos. interest to date	1,030	
June	10	Balance	551	74		1900				
						May	15	6 mos. interest to date	1,030	
			2,301	74					2,301	74
						June	10	Balance	551	74

(13) TRANSFER TAX

1899						1899				
Apr.	19	Cash	2,463	83		Apr.	19	Personal est. account	2,463	83

(14) EXPENSES OF REALIZATION AND ADMINISTRATION

1900						1900				
June	10	Commission	250			June	10	Cash	250	
		Legal expenses	375	87				"	375	87
		Miscellaneous	50					"	50	
			675	87					675	87

(15) TRIAL BALANCE 20TH JUNE, 1900

	Cash	1,210	74			Life beneficiary estate	551	74
	Household furniture	2,000				Personal est. account	54,159	
	Mortgages receivable	51,500						
		54,710	74				54,710	74

ACCOUNT OF CHARGE AND DISCHARGE OF MANAGEMENT
Death of Testator, 31st March, 1899

		————— CHARGE —————					
	I	FOR ACCOUNT OF CAPITAL					
1899 Apr.	4	Estate as given in inventory:—					
		Cash in Bank				250	
		Household furniture				2,000	
		Bank shares				45,250	
		Life insurance policy				15,000	
		On deposit with Trust Co. Deposit		2,000		2,019	29
		Interest to date		19	29		
		Rents due and unpaid				1,250	
						65,769	29
		Funds and Estate realized:—	Inventory	Realiz-	ed		
Apr.	1	Cash in Bank	250	250			
	18	Amount of life insurance policy	15,000	15,000			
May	13	Proceeds of sale of Bank shares	45,250	45,775			
	14	Deposit in Trust Company	2,019.29	2,025	41		
	15	Rents due and unpaid	1,250	1,250			
			63,769.29	64,300	41		
				63,769	29		
		Gross gain including income		531	12		
		Less portion belonging to income:—					
		Portion of dividend on Bank shares held from 31st March, 1899, to 13th May, 1899	235.62				
		Interest on deposit in Trust Co. from 31st March, 1899, to 14th May, 1900	6.12	241	74	289	38
		Total Capital realized				66,058	67
1899 May	15	Rents received:—					
		From Andrew Mason		375			
		Wm. J. Renall		500			
		Mary Hoskins		375			
		John Hardy		250			
				1,500			
		Less rents belong to capital paid as above		1,250			
				250			
		Paid John Hoskins, sole heir		250		00,000	00
						66,058	67
1899 Nov.	15	For account income:—					
		6 months' interest on mortgage on No. 40 W. 28th St., to date		1,030			
1900 May	15	6 months' interest on mortgage on No. 40 W. 28th St., to date		1,030			
				2,060			
		Add: Portion of dividend of bank shares contained in selling price from 31st March, 1899, to 15th May, 1899	235.62				
		Interest on deposit in Trust Co. from 31st March, 1899, to 14th May, 1899	6.12	241	74	2,301	74
		Total of charge				68,360	41
		REAL ESTATE					
		By terms of Trust Deed this property has been conveyed by Trustee to John Hoskins, son of decedent, and is valued at	45,000				

OF THE Executor and Trustee of Estate of John Hoskins
Death of L. B., 14th May, 1900.

	I	———————————DISCHARGE———————						
		PAYMENTS OUT OF CAPITAL						
1899 Apl.	19	1. Funeral expenses					150	
		2. Debts due by deceased:—						
		Dr. Sampson's bill	52	50				
		Servants' wages	150					
		A. Langstadter's bill	75	12				
		William Anderson's bill	2,656	25				
		Daniel Tompson's bill	60	62				
		John Harris' bill	272	62				
		William Fife's bill	85	62				
		Brooks Bros' bill	105	12				
		Acker, Merrill & Condit's bill	152	12				
				—			3,609	97
		3. Transfer tax					2,463	83
June	10	4. Legacy paid					5,000	
1900 June	10	5. Expenses of realization and administration:—						
		Commission to executor	250					
		Legal expenses	375	87				
		Miscellaneous expenses	50				675	87
		Total, payments out of capital					11,899	67
	II	**PAYMENTS OUT OF INCOME**						
1899 May	12	1. Payments to life beneficiary:—						
		Paid life beneficiary on account	750					
1900 May	12	Paid life beneficiary on account	1,000				1,750	
						—	13,649	67
		2. Expenses of management and other charges					00,000	00
	III	Estate as of 10th June, 1900;—						
		Mortgage on No. 40 West 28th St., N. Y.	51,500					
		Household furniture	2,000					
		Cash in Bank	1,210	74				
				—			54,710	74
				—			68,360	41
1899 May	15	**INVESTMENTS MADE** Made loan this day, secured by mortgage on No. 40 W. 28th St., N. Y., at 4 per cent. per annum 51,500						

ANOTHER FORM BY MEANS OF SCHEDULES

1899		**I. INCOME RECEIVED**				
May	13	For life beneficiary's portion of dividend on Bank shares from 31st March, 1899, to date	235	62		
Nov.	15	6 months' interest to date on mortgage on No. 40 W. 28th St., N. Y.	1,030			
1900						
May	14	Interest on deposit in Trust Co. from 31st March, 1899, to date	6	12		
	15	6 months' interest to date on mortgage on No. 40 W. 28th St., N. Y.	1,030	—	2,301	74
		II. INCOME PAID				
		None	0,000	00	0,000	00
		Summary of income:—				
		Income received	2,301	74		
		Income paid	0,000	00	2,301	74
		Amount paid life beneficiary:—				
1899						
May	12	Cash paid life beneficiary on account	750			
1900						
May	12	Cash paid life beneficiary on account	1,000			
June	10	Amount due life beneficiary	551	74	2,301	74
		III. CHANGES IN INVESTMENTS				
		Inventory:—				
		Cash	250			
		Life insurance policy	15,000			
		Bank shares	45,250			
		Deposit in Trust Company	2,019	29		
		Rent due and unpaid	1,250			
		Household furniture	2,000		65,769	29
1900						
June	10	Assets realized:—				
		Cash on hand	250			
		Sale of Bank shares:— Sale 45,775				
		Less accrued dividend 235.62	45,539	38		
		Household furniture	2,000			
		Amount of life insurance policy	15,000			
		Withdrawn from Trust Co.				
		Withdrawn 2,025.41	,			
		Less interest 6.12	2,019	29		
		Received rent due and unpaid	1,250	—	66,058	67
		Less inventory value as above			65,769	29
		Increase of assets			289	38
		IV. ADDITIONS TO PRINCIPAL	0,000	00		

1900							
June	10	**V. DEDUCTION FROM PRINCIPAL**					
		Charges against reminderman:—					
		Dr Sampson's bill	52.50				
		Servants' wages	150				
		A. Langstadter's bill	75.12				
		William Anderson's loan to decedent	2,656.25				
		John Harris' bill	272.62				
		Daniel Tompson's bill	60.62				
		Wm Fife's bill	85.62				
		Brooks Bros.' bill	105.12				
		Acker, Merrill & Condit's bill	152.12	3,609	97		
		Funeral expenses, Undertaker's bill		150			
		Transfer tax		2,463	83		
		Legacy to Mary Hoskins		5,000			
				11,223	80		
		Expenses in realization and administration:—					
		Commission	250				
		Legal expenses	375.87				
		Miscellaneous expenses	50	675	87	11,899	67
		VI. PRINCIPAL ON HAND					
		Cash:— Cash on hand	1,210.74				
		Less due life beneficiary	551.74	659			
		Household furniture		2,000			
		Mortgage on No. 40 W. 28th St., N. Y.		51,500		54,159	
		Summary of principal:—					
		Inventory		65,769	29		
		Increase from transfers		289	38		
		Addition to principal		000	00	66,058	67
		Less deductions from principal				11,899	67
		Net total principal				54,195	

9 781331 523703